PUSH YOUR WAY TO PURPOSE

ALSO BY ADRIENNE ROSS

#AuntAlma: Raisin' a Little ~~Hell~~ Heaven on Earth

#AuntAlma Unleashed: Old, Bold, and Out of Control

PUSH YOUR WAY TO PURPOSE

*How to Get from Where You Are
to Where You're Meant to Be*

ADRIENNE ROSS

ARC Publishing

PUSH YOUR WAY TO PURPOSE

© 2017 by Adrienne Ross

Published by ARC Publishing
P.O. Box 173
Jackson, Missouri 63755

Cover design by Mary Pat King Creative Design:
marypatking.com
Author photographs by Cheekwood Studio:
cheekwoodstudio.com

Visit the author's websites: adriennerosscom.com and auntalma.com.

This book is dedicated to my mother, Jeanette Ross.
I cannot think of a time
when you did not believe
I could accomplish anything I wanted.
Those words you spoke to me repeatedly in my
earliest years—
"Adrienne, you talk from the time you wake up to the
time you go to sleep!"—
have remained with me.
I'm still talking,
and this voice has served me well!
You were my first love, Mom,
and I thank you.

CONTENTS

Acknowledgments
Introduction

1. Name Your Purpose   1
2. Mommy, I Can't Want To   13
3. Finish What You Start   21
4. Discover Your Purpose   33
5. Use the F-Word   43
6. Toolbox for Success   55
7. Lessons from the Sideline: It's Hard   71
8. Raise Your Expectations   85
9. She Killed Herself   109
10. Familiar Territory   125
11. Be Open   135

Final Thoughts
Meet the Author
Contact the Author

ACKNOWLEDGMENTS

Thank You, Jesus. Your amazing grace and unconditional love have saved me. You are my reason for everything.

Kristi King, thank you for encouraging me to write this book. I would have missed this humbling opportunity without your insistence.

Kiya Cordeau, you confirmed that I needed to write a motivational book. Thank you. Our friendship is a gift from God.

Thank you, Cherie Cordeau, for providing the inspiration for one of the most powerful chapters and life-lessons within these pages.

Thank you, Lakia Walker and Carthette Burnett, sisters to one another who have become sisters to me. Your faith in me, support, and prayers are unparalleled. I see characteristics of your mother in both of you.

All my family and friends, I thank you for walking alongside me. We get to do life together, and I am a stronger person because of you.

Thank you, Hudson City School District. For more than 17 years, you gave me the opportunity to teach some of the most amazing students with some of the most wonderful colleagues. Many of the principles in this book stem from that time and those experiences. My gratitude abounds.

Thank you, pastors and members of the congregations I have been honored to call my church homes throughout the years, especially Rock Solid Church, River of Life International, and Christ Church of the Heartland. You have believed in me, prayed for me, and spoken words of life over me. Qualities from each of you live in me, and I am grateful I get to share them with others.

INTRODUCTION

Purpose consumes me. It always has. *Who are you? Why are you? What will you?* I began contemplating those questions when I was a young girl sitting in my bedroom and staring at pictures of music and television icons taped to my wall. But it started long before that. I entered the world with a mandate on my life. It was spoken. It was so. But I didn't know.

I always had a feeling that something larger was calling me, though, which made little sense, considering that I lived in rather ordinary surroundings. The projects of the Bronx don't exactly conjure up images of greatness. Later, after I moved to Long Island, a bright future may have seemed more likely to the onlooker—like I was getting closer to the possibility of greatness, but even as I daydreamed, there was a nagging longing for more. But how would I make it happen?

Isn't that the question everyone asks? If you think not, think again. By 11, children have already begun wondering what their purpose is. By 40, adults have begun wondering if they missed theirs. We're all consumed with purpose. Your neighbors are. Your co-workers are. You are. We may not recognize it, but it's there—in the words we speak, the decisions we make, even the friends we keep. Everything points back to purpose and our longing for it.

What are the odds that we will fulfill our purpose, though? The answer has everything to do with identity, being able to recognize who we truly are. Unfortunately, many never come to this revelation. As a result, they live beneath themselves. Even those seemingly on top of the world struggle with identity.

I am writing this book because I have a message to share, one that will help you understand that there's more waiting—for you. No matter how low you've fallen or how high you've climbed, you're marked for more.

This isn't one of those name it, claim it, blab it, grab it, sprinkle a little dust, and you can have it self-help books meant to pump you up with hot air. Those books do pump you up, right before dropping you—on your head. This book doesn't tell you that reaching the place you were meant to be is 1-2-3 easy. In fact, it tells you the opposite. Some of it is difficult, but all of it is doable. My experiences provide keys to unlock the doors to your destiny and introduce you to life-changing principles. My book is called *Push Your Way to Purpose* for a reason. Let's just say the title also has a purpose. "Push" is a verb. Verbs are action words. You have to become a verb to grasp what the book's subtitle promises to teach you: *How to Get from Where You Are to Where You're Meant to Be.*

Nobody wants to push anymore. We want everything to be easy. But easy doesn't bring us to destiny. I don't believe it was supposed to be as hard as we have made it, though. God created us with basic instructions: BE. But "but" got in the way. We "but"-ed our way out of "be," making excuses for being everything other than our best, and we made messes along the way. Some messes look like successes, while other messes can't hide. Some people are so far down they can't even imagine up. But most of the people we encounter are just your ordinary, go-along-to-get-along people. They're not at rock bottom, and they're not soaring on the clouds. They're average, working, normal people. They're parents, teachers, students, friends. They're community members you see in the supermarket. They run for elected office. They change diapers. They're you. They're me.

So we're in this together. We each have a purpose, and we can discover it, then fulfill it. It will require effort, a willingness never to settle for less than who we are meant to be. It may also require swallowing our egos. if we think we have it all together and embracing our potential if we think we have nothing together. Wherever we sit on that spectrum, let us get up, raise our expectations, believe for more, and push our way to purpose. It's time.

CHAPTER 1

NAME YOUR PURPOSE

"**N**ame her Adrienne because she's going to be a schoolteacher." I've shared this story more times than I can count, and for good reason: by the time I'm done telling the story, it always garners the desired response. What is that story, and what is the response? That's the purpose of this chapter. It's a perfect place to start because it sets the stage for the focus of this book.

Everyone wants to be successful. Everyone wants to believe that she was, in fact, born to be successful, that the age-old adage is true for her life: "The sky is the limit." Some would bet the farm—or the high-rise —on it. It sounds good, doesn't it? But it's not true, or at least it's not necessarily true. Like most things, it must be made to be true. You have to grab it and make it true in your life. The sky very well may be the limit, but so may the floor. It all depends on the level of your reach, the things you've chosen to embrace, the relationships you have—and have not—fostered. All these and more figure into your limit. You may be one of those whose life seems to be without limits, or you may be one who seemingly cannot catch a break. It could go either way because while there are circumstances that are beyond our control and you-know-what sometimes just happens, very often, the thing that happens to us *is* us.

One thing influencing our level of success is what we hear. When I say "hear," I mean "listen to." Many words bump into my ear in the course of a day, but I don't feed off of them all. There's a huge difference between what I hear well enough to repeat and what I listen to and choose to eat—to digest. *I* decide. And it makes all the difference in the world.

The story I referenced is that when I was born, Aunt Mary, my dad's oldest sister, said to my mother, "Name her Adrienne because she's going to be a schoolteacher." If you're like me, you're thinking, "What in the world does the name Adrienne have to do with being a teacher?" It makes zero sense to me, too, but apparently, it made sense to my aunt. Maybe to her Adrienne just sounded like a "smart" name.

Aunt Mary was good for using the word "smart" to describe all sorts of things. "I'll buy you these sneakers right here. Don't they look smart?" Yeah, they looked smart all right, which is why I wanted to get as far away from them suckers as possible! If you were anywhere below the age of 40, "smart" was code for "butt-ugly," "all the kids are gonna laugh at you," and "run for the door." Considering that description, I hate to think I looked "smart" at birth, so there had to be another reason for the connection.

Whatever Aunt Mary was thinking, she had made the pronouncement: Adrienne was going to be a teacher.

I share this story when I speak to audiences because it highlights the power of words. I did go on to become a teacher. I was an English Language Arts teacher for more than 17 years in Hudson, New York. I didn't embrace my destiny right away, though all my life, I was clearly well-suited to be an English teacher. It wasn't until I had almost completed college that I decided to go that route. All my life, I loved writing and speaking, but teaching young people? Are you kidding me? No way! I was going to be an actress. I later learned that teaching great literature was not much different from performing on stage, so I got the

3

best of both worlds when I did enter the education profession.

When I consider the power of words, I realize that my aunt could very well have said, "Name her Adrienne—or Darlene, or Shaniqua, or whatever— because she's going to be a big nobody." That could have been the prophetic utterance that became a curse over me. And yes, I do mean curse. I cannot believe in the Bible and not believe in curses and blessings, and I do believe in the Bible. The spoken word is one way blessings and curses are released upon us. My aunt spoke a blessing over me, though growing up, I did not deem being a teacher anything but a curse. How could spending hour upon hour with smart aleck kids be anything else?

Let me be upfront. Aunt Mary was no angel, she did not always speak glowing words over me, and at times, the words she did speak hurt. So I do not want to paint a picture of a perfect human being who spoke perfect words at the perfect time all the time, thereby molding me into this perfect person. No, she was an imperfect person who happened to help raise another imperfect person—one who faced challenges, benefited from God's grace, and embraced her destiny.

My mother, too, was instrumental in shaping my life. For a moment, I had ambitions of being a crossing guard. Don't even ask where that came from. Don't get me wrong: being able to keep up with a group of kids and get them across the street safely is no easy task, but I was going to do it.

I had to do the famous "What I Want to Be When I Grow Up" homework assignment, probably in the third grade. My mom was lying in her bed, and I showed her what I had written. Upon reading it, she said, "You don't want to be a crossing guard. Write that you want to be a singer."

Well, Mommy said it, and it sounded good to me, so for some time, I wanted to be a singer. Of all the time that I had that dream, there's only one song I remember wanting to sing. I loved the song "I Will Survive" by Gloria Gaynor, and I had plans to do a remake of it one day.

Other than the crossing guard idea, which lasted all of about an hour, and then the pursuit in later years to become a teacher, I've never wanted to be anything ordinary. I'm not sure there is such a thing as ordinary because everything we do is what we make it. Everything we do is ministry. So in reality, there is no ordinary. Our life's work is as extraordinary as we make it. My point, though, is that almost every dream I've ever had involved something that seemed far-fetched, the kind of things about which people say, "Make sure you have a backup plan because only one in a zillion ever make it doing that." Let's see: I've wanted to be a singer, an actress, a talk show host, and a writer. And while I've never wanted to be President of the United States, I still have thoughts of being a press secretary or speechwriter for a president, but that's a story for another book.

For most of my life, I have carried in my spirit a feeling about my future, about my purpose. I could never find words to express it, and it's probably a good thing because when I was finally able to put my finger on it, I realized it's one of those things you don't tell just anybody.

Years ago, I was listening to a cassette. If you're younger than 35, you probably think that's a name: Cassette Angelina Johnson or some similar combination. No, not Cassette. cassette. It's this thing in the shape of a square with a roll of tape inside. You stick the square into this box called a radio and hit Play, and, if the tape does not get stuck and rip or get pulled out into a wad on the floor, it'll play back what someone recorded. If it does get pulled out, don't fear:

pencils are quite handy at reeling the tape back in, and if it rips, a little piece of adhesive tape placed ever so precisely usually does the trick. But I digress. "What's a pencil?" you ask. It's long, thin, usually yellow. Never mind; go back to your iPad.

Anyway, I had been driving my car, listening to Oprah Winfrey on that cassette as she gave a speech. I couldn't tell you today the topic of her speech. I only remember her saying that she always felt she was destined for greatness. Those were probably not her exact words, but that's what she was saying. And when she said it, something arose within me, a light bulb came on, and I exclaimed, "That's it! That's what I've been feeling!" And that was it indeed. I had a certain something-something in me for years, but I didn't know what it was—until I heard Oprah say it. When she did, something exploded inside. There's this saying in the church: "Some things are taught, but some things are caught." That means there are things we learn and grasp intellectually, but there are some things that are larger than that. They're things we need a revelation of, things that don't ask the brain for permission to understand because the heart already grasped them. What Oprah said hit me like a ton of bricks. I finally saw the light—and it emanated from

Oprah Winfrey—someone I grew up admiring and wanting to emulate. I don't rush home anymore to watch her on television or sit with mouth agape hanging on her every word. But at that time, she served a purpose in my life, and for that, I'm grateful.

One summer, I was reading a series in which the main character was a teacher. I stole an idea from that book to use in my own classroom in the fast-approaching school year. I went to school and got the attendance rosters for each of my classes, as up-to-date as I could manage. I spent hours sitting at my computer pondering the names of those students who would walk into my classroom in a couple of weeks. I researched the meanings and origins of those names. I bought decorative stationery onto which I printed the names and meanings, along with declarations about their lives—the greatness they epitomized as foretold by their names. I took each of those papers to Staples for them to cut and laminate.

The first week of school brought a conferment ceremony to my students. In each of my classes, I stood behind a podium, called each person individually to the front, declared his/her name and its meaning, and spoke a powerful message that corresponded to that name. In other words, I conferred the meanings of their names upon them and charged them to live that out. Every day, students brought that laminated prophecy—which is how I saw it—because they kept it in the pocket of their binders. I told them that when times got tough or when they were underachieving, I was going to call their attention to that paper and who they were—what their names said about them—not what their circumstances said about them. Together, we would believe the best in and for them.

That project was both joyful and challenging. Some names were a piece of cake. I mean, when a person's name means "Messenger of God," it's rather easy to come up with a positive pronouncement: "You are blessed. You will speak with authority, and people will listen. Your voice will make a difference for good in this world." The possibilities are endless. When a name means "swamp," however, it takes a bit more creativity to come up with something that will instill a feeling of purpose and pride in a person. In a case like that, I resorted to something similar to: "A swamp is a place where things grow. It's green because it teems with life. You, too, teem with life and will produce great things."

The ceremony was a small thing, yet it was big. It was a way to get students to understand their potential, to embrace who they were and what they could do, and to challenge them to live up to that. It also gave me something to draw their attention back to when they were inclined to be less than their best. Kids are kids, and they're going to make mistakes and not always demonstrate the power to do good or the call to uplift those around them. But they also don't forget easily. I believed that as I spoke their names over them and handed them those papers, something was set in motion that would impact their lives in ways they would not even realize until years later.

I was able to do this with my students' names because I was living what was spoken over me when I was named: "Name her Adrienne because she's going to be a schoolteacher." You have to laugh and wonder exactly what enabled Aunt Mary to see what she did. She sure did see it, though, didn't she? She had a vision for my purpose, and she gave it a name.

Much went into making me the person I am today. But it wasn't all rosy. Not everyone believed in me, and I didn't always believe in myself. Life sucks sometimes, people, and the sooner we realize that, the sooner we can adjust to it and deal with it. Even those who love us most are not always our biggest cheerleaders, so we'd better have something within ourselves to keep us moving forward.

CHAPTER 2

MOMMY, I CAN'T WANT TO

When Cherie was a toddler, her response to many of her mother's requests was, "But I can't want to."

"Cherie, please pick up that toy."

"Mommy, I can't want to."

"Cherie, eat that last piece of broccoli."

"But Mommy, I can't want to. I can't want to, Mommy."

I love it! Who says, "I can't want to"? I mean, "I *don't* want to." "I *won't*." "Get lost!" But "I can't want to"?

I'm pretty sure it was all Cherie's mother and father could do not to laugh and give in. But they had to keep it together to get the point across: "Cherie, you have to do what we tell you."

Giving in would not have taught Cherie the life-lesson that every productive member of society must learn—that even when you can't want to, you've got to. There are things you just have to do. The difference between winners and losers in life is often very simple. Those who succeed are those who find the strength to do what they can't want to do to get the results they do want to get.

I have played basketball most of my life. In high school, I spent many years as a benchwarmer, but senior year was my year. I was team captain, a fierce defender, a good three-point shooter, and a decent point guard. All the stars, including my sister, Mona, had graduated, and I was feeling this new role big time. I logged lots of minutes—hardly coming out of games; Coach Pollack needed me on the floor.

Now, I loved playing basketball. My sister and I would play all year. Even in the winter, we'd be on a court somewhere—snow on the ground and all. I have played basketball so long that I cannot remember when I first picked up a ball. But I also remember the exertion of playing games and hardly ever coming out to rest. I described it as my body being on fire. It hurt so much, and at times, I would say, "I hate what this feels like." I also had a knee injury to contend with and the all-too-frequent jammed fingers. I played three sports, and it wasn't always easy being an athlete. But where was I every day? At practice or a game. Oh, there were times I couldn't want to, but I did it anyway—for the love of the game, for the victories—which, by the way, were few and far between. And because I did it, as an adult, I was able to coach others, and I can still beat many a grown man in this game called basketball. Had I walked away when I couldn't want to, I would have missed out on fun times, learning experiences, and valuable relationships.

I couldn't want to go back to college for my master's degree, either. Shortly after college, I got a job I despised. It was one of those situations where management treated you like a nobody, and you wanted to tell them you were destined for greatness but figured that wouldn't go over too well, so you kept your mouth shut and told them off—to your friends. Yes, one of those jobs.

I was not particularly interested in another two years of college, but by the end of my undergraduate studies, I had embraced my calling to teach. I knew I would have to have a master's to do so. I knew, too, that I would need to take out some loans, which I also could not want to do. Aunt Mary's sister, Aunt Alma, told me, "You either take out a loan now and pay it back when you've got the money to do so because you have your degree, or you spend a lifetime making less money because you didn't take out a loan to make more money." Aunt Alma was my favorite aunt, and I respected her opinion. We could have a conversation today about the wisdom—or lack thereof—of her advice, but it worked for me, so it's serviceable at this time.

Another thing I couldn't want to do is watch Aunt Mary in the last year of her life. She had suffered cardiac arrest, which rendered her unable to talk, walk, or even move on her own. It was a freak situation in which she had fallen and broken a hip. That, of course, was bad enough for a woman in her seventies, but it wasn't supposed to turn into what it did. She was a diabetic and went to dialysis three times a week. Aunt Alma had basically moved in with her and Uncle Cleveland to help take care of Aunt Mary prior to the cardiac arrest. This was before my uncle unexpectedly passed away more than a year before Aunt Mary.

When her sister suffered cardiac arrest, Aunt Alma spent all day, every day, at the hospital, right by her side. It was hard for her to see her sister that way, and it was hard to leave her side. No one wants to see a loved one lying in a bed, not conscious at first, then regaining consciousness eventually, yet still unable to communicate. We weren't even sure how much brain activity there was, how much Aunt Mary understood. The healthcare professionals had to turn her regularly to try to keep her from getting bed sores. She also had a tracheotomy, and the area had to be periodically suctioned. She could not tell us when she went to the bathroom in her pampers, so we had to be on the lookout for that. You cannot understand what it's like seeing someone you love in that condition unless you've experienced it. It's heartrending.

I lived three hours away and was teaching every day, but on the weekends, I got in the car, drove to Long Island, and spent Saturdays there, from late mornings to about 11 o'clock at night. I went back to the nursing home the next morning, stayed until the afternoon, then drove the three hours back Upstate. I went to work on Monday mornings and did it all over again at the end of the week. This was the routine for more than a year. Many times, I couldn't want to. I took students' papers to Long Island to grade, but it was difficult to get work done there. I always had my laptop with me to do some writing, as I was heavy into blogging, but focusing was a challenge. I did it anyway. I did it for Aunt Mary because she had raised me. She had sacrificed for me. She had, no doubt, done many things she couldn't want to throughout the years because she loved me. In fact, she had spent much of her life looking after others and doing the things that needed to be done for that reason—because they needed to be done. I also did it for Aunt Alma. In fact, I may have done it more for her than Aunt Mary. Aunt Alma was wearing herself out, and if you saw her working the staff over at the nursing home, you knew that she was wearing them out also. When I came on the weekends, everybody got a break! I wanted my aunt to get some rest, get some things done, try to be somewhat normal in the midst of this tragedy that was anything but normal. I knew that if I were not there to give her a respite, she would never leave that place. So I did what I had to do, just as Aunt Alma did what she had to do.

My point is that none of us can want to do many things, and at times, we face things that make us feel like those little kids we once were. Oh, how we wish we could go back in time, look at the adult in our lives who shouldered all the responsibility, and say, like

Cherie, "But Mommy, I can't want to." But it's like the Bible says, "When I was a child, I spoke as a child, I understood as a child, I thought as a child; but when I became a man, I put away childish things."

"I can't want to" is a childish thing. It may be funny or cute and may even work when a toddler says it, but it's just not going to fly when we're older. So I advise young people to do what they have to do—no matter how they feel. It's not about feelings. Feelings lie. Feelings change. Feelings cause trouble. Responsibility exists no matter how we feel. And what is responsibility? A graduate school professor wrote on one of my papers, "Responsibility is the ability to respond." We have that ability.

So you can't want to. That's okay. Do it anyway. Persevere. People who can move ahead even when they don't feel like moving at all are people who will experience much more success than people who realize they can't want to and so they don't. Even Cherie outgrew "But I can't want to." Look, everyone has a "but," an excuse not to achieve more. Push past yours so you can fulfill your purpose.

CHAPTER 3

FINISH WHAT YOU START

I am Adrienne, professional starter. I can start almost anything: reading a book, writing a book, planning an event. I'm rather good at it. It's the finishing that I struggle with. At least that's the way it's been for a big chunk of my existence. I'll get great ideas, make some preliminary actions, and then drop the ball somewhere along the way. I could be wrong, but I don't think I'm alone in that. I think most people are the same way. We mean well, but we find ourselves thrown off course.

So what gets us off course? That's a question we must answer if we're ever to overcome that flaw. And yes, it is a flaw. Often, we excuse flaws by denying that they really are flaws. We call them personality traits or say, "That's just the way I am" and "It is what it is." Well, what it *is* is a flaw that robs us of our potential.

We think of a graveyard as a place filled with dead bodies. It is. But more than that, a graveyard is filled with dead dreams, dead ambitions, and dead potential. "You can't take it with you," the old saying, isn't true. Many people take what could have been to the cemetery with them.

I cannot count the number of books I started writing. They were good, too: fiction, non-fiction, an autobiography or two, plays, poems, you name it. But when I decided to write *#AuntAlma: Raisin' a Little ~~Hell~~ Heaven on Earth*, I knew I wanted to complete it. It was both an answer to popular demand and a tribute to my aunt, a book of colorful illustrations, quotations, and stories. It required my hiring an illustrator. I knew I did not pay that kind of money to quit. But even so, even after the illustrator had done his part and had delivered the images to me, I still procrastinated in doing what I had yet to do. I still had to write the stories for the various quotations. I had to decide what route to take for publication—self-publishing or traditional publishing. I had to push through an already-packed schedule to find the time to get it all done. It was easier to let it sit. I had started it, and most of the work was complete, but I had to take more steps.

My illustrator, John, and I had started collaborating on the images in April, and he had finished them in November. Almost six months later, I had not completed my stories or decided how I wanted to market my book. Sure, I had started the story writing, but what else is new? Remember, I was a professional starter.

I am a part of a 6:30 a.m. weekly Bible study called The Tree. It's tailored for Christian businessmen and businesswomen. At one of these studies, Pastor Adrian Taylor uttered a phrase that resonated with me and changed everything. He said, simply, "Finish what you start." It wasn't the topic of the study, but it found its way into what he was teaching. Two things came to mind when I heard that. One thing was that I hadn't finished reading the book he had written. I had started it months prior, enjoyed what I had read, but had never resumed reading. I determined that day that I would finish reading his book. The second thing was that I would finish writing my own book. In days, I finished his book. No more than a few days after that, I put the finishing touches on my book.

Now, before this, I wasn't sure how I wanted to proceed with publishing. It seemed like the "right" thing to get my book into the hands of a traditional publisher to give it more legitimacy—or so some people think. But I sought some wisdom from Pastor Adrian about his book. In so doing, I learned more about self-publishing. I followed up with another friend who had self-published several books. I made up my mind. Once I determined to move ahead, that I was no longer going to wait it out, that it was time to finish what I started, I decided to take responsibility for my own book and my own success. I demonstrated what my graduate school professor called the ability to respond, and I responded to the inner urging to finish what I started by self-publishing. I did not want to wait 12 months or 16 months to get my book into the hands of people who were hungry for it. Once I decided to move ahead, I was ready to roll. I did my research, and I did my due diligence. Adrienne's success or failure was going to fall on Adrienne. I realized that the marketing would be on me, the book signing events would be on me, and the end results would be on me—and I was fine with that. I was done waiting.

So I finished what I started. On May 17, 2016, I published my book. I started marketing it, and people started buying it.

I wanted to do a Barnes & Noble book signing, which isn't easy when you're self-published. I sought advice, and not only did I get advice from a prominent member of our community, Gary Rust, who owns the *Southeast Missourian* newspaper, where I sit on the editorial board and write a weekly column, but I received incredible support from the paper—a commitment to back my efforts with advertising. The *Missourian* team devised a plan centered around my success. Gary also suggested what was already in my heart: go to Barnes & Noble. He said to let them know the paper would stand behind me.

I walked into that bookstore with a copy of my book, spoke to one of the managers, and learned how difficult it was to secure a book signing when you don't have HarperCollins or Simon & Schuster imprinted on your book, but I also learned the power of perseverance. It took some time, and though I was told "no" at one point, that "no" eventually turned to "yes." I signed a contract with Barnes & Noble, and little ol' Adrienne was about to have a book signing in the store where she spent hours over the years buying and reading other people's books! I had to be flexible, yes, but hey, I could do that. I had to do it through consignment, meaning I purchased my own books, took them there, and left with whatever didn't sell. Again, my success or failure was on me. As scary as that may seem, isn't that a good way to do it? Yes, it's frightening: What if no one showed up? After telling Barnes & Noble that I wouldn't disappoint, what if I did?

But then, what if I didn't? And guess what: I didn't. It was a success in every way. But it would not have been if I had not finished what I started—worked with an illustrator; gathered quotes; wrote stories; pursued the mecca of bookstores after it turned me down; mailed out invitations; marketed my book; and the rest of it. But it all picked up speed because of one phrase that I heard with my ears and responded to with my heart and my actions: finish what you start.

What would you accomplish if you picked up the things you started but dropped? How many books would you write? How much money would you save? How many friendships would you develop? The truth is there is a treasure within us, and when we fail to release it, we rob not only ourselves, but we rob our families, our communities, our nation, and the world of what we were meant to invest. "Come on now," you say. "It's not that serious." But it is that serious. What's more serious than doing the thing you are here to do? What's more serious than fulfilling your purpose—impacting your life and the lives of others? And what would be sadder than getting to the end of your journey and realizing that you settled for less because you refused to finish what you started? You had the resources. All you had to do was put them to work, push a little bit, be a little uncomfortable at times to achieve success and greatness and to fulfill your purpose.

And what are success and greatness? That's a question many don't know how to answer, but I do. It's not what people think it is. Most people would point to the famous Hollywood actor, the runway model, the billion-dollar businessman. They would say, "That's success right there." Wrong. Well, not completely. What you must understand is that success is different for different people. "So how do I determine if I'm a success?" you wisely ask—and I'm glad you did because you need to have that question answered.

Success is doing what you've been created to do. When a woodworker carves out a beautiful chair so his household guests have a place to sit, completes it, sits down on it, and the chair holds him up, that chair is a success. That chair is fulfilling its purpose. That's what it was made for. That's why the creator created it. If the chair, however, crumbles into a heap on the floor or is only sturdy enough to lean against the wall or manages to hold a few magazines, that chair is not a success. "But it's so beautiful," you say. It doesn't matter how beautiful it is; the chair has underperformed. Nonetheless, people get it twisted. Sometimes, they're stuck on the beauty of the chair or that it can do other things like hold magazines or even that it matches the room's decor. It's good enough, they feel. But that's not the point. The woodworker didn't set out to create something good enough. He set out to create a chair that would fulfill a specific purpose. Now, he can, as they say, "make do," but that wasn't the plan—and now, his guests are deprived of that chair they needed to sit in. The loss of purpose had far-reaching consequences.

This is how many of us approach life. First, we sell out that thing we should do, perhaps that thing we started but allowed to just crumble into one big heap on the floor. We settle. Why? Because it got hard or got long or we just got weary. So maybe we do something else, and maybe we're good at it. Maybe we look beautiful doing it, too. In fact, it's going so well, we don't even realize that we're "making do." Add to that the people who praise us as we do this other thing, who only know us in that role, and who think we're hot stuff doing it. Hear me: we may totally rock at it. Others may be blessed by it. But that is not how we measure success.

I have heard happily married couples herald marriage as the best thing in the world, and trust me, I believe in marriage. I believe God ordained it. I believe it is a holy institution. But marriage is not the best thing in the world. Neither is being single, though people who praise its freedom declare that it is. They get to go and come as they please, not answering to anyone. This is the life! Wrong again. So now you're confused. Which is it? What's the best thing in the world—marriage or singleness? Neither. And both. For the person called to be married, marriage is the best thing in the world. For the person not called to be married, it's hell. For the person called to be single, singleness is the best thing in the world. For the person not called to be single, singleness is hell. See, it's about fulfilling your purpose. It's about doing what you've been called to do. That's where contentment, peace, and joy reside. So are you saying, Adrienne, that someone can have Bill Gates status and not be successful? You're getting it! But that's billions of dollars. That's prestige. That's influence. Yes, and if you're called to do that, that's success. But if you're not called to do that, that's not. If you were called to work with special needs students in a private school in the middle of nowhere, and instead of embracing and completing your mission, you opted to follow in Bill Gates' footsteps, you have not achieved success.

We're always trying to define success, and it's so simple. You've been waiting all your life to find out what success is, and I'm going to end your search right here. Success is simply doing what you're supposed to do when you're supposed to do it.

Knowing the definition and living it are two different things, however. Many struggle with how to know what they are supposed to do, and we'll deal with that in the next chapter.

For now, endure the self-reflection and create your list of the things you have started that you are certain —even somewhat certain—you were to complete. Should you pick them up again? Should you take the advice that I took, advice that set significant things in motion for me? Are you tired of being the professional starter that I was—good at taking off but really bad at crossing the finish line? It all comes down to finishing what you started. Should you do it? If so, what's holding you back?

CHAPTER 4

DISCOVER YOUR PURPOSE

"Why am I here?" is not just some deep philosophical question meant for scholars and religious leaders. It's a question every soul asks. As a teacher, I found that students as young as 11 and 12 had already begun asking themselves this. Sometimes, we phrase it differently. Sometimes, the best way we can express it is, "What do I want to be when I grow up?" But the spirit behind it is about purpose, about why I am here, about what I'm supposed to be doing while I'm here. It's a wise consideration, too. While we should not allow the discovery to consume us to the point of discontent, we should care about our purpose. We should know that we're not here by accident, and since that's the case, there is purpose for our being here. Accident is the opposite of purpose, right? Isn't that what we say? "I'm sorry. I didn't do it on purpose. It was an accident." Well, an accident involving dropping a dish and breaking it is one thing, but an accident involving the direction one's life goes is another. We all want to feel like what we do matters, and the older we get, it seems, the more we want to make sure we're doing it right.

Some people have known all their lives what it is they were meant to be. "I always knew I would be a missionary," you might hear someone say, or you hear, "I was in my forties and realized that my true gift was baking, so I opened up a bakery." However it pans out, there are clues that reveal our life's purpose. I often highlight three of them.

What Do You Love?

The thing that makes you the happiest can be the number one clue to your purpose. That sounds too good to be true, right? I mean, if I love it that much, it should be my hobby—the thing I do if I can find the time to squeeze it in. Why do we think like that? Why do we embrace the crazy idea that if we love it too much, it's too good to be true? Imagine if basketball legend Michael Jordan thought like that or *Diary of a Wimpy Kid* author, Jeff Kinney, thought like that? *We* would be without things we love because *they* brushed off the things they loved or relegated them to mere hobbies rather than their professions—their investment into society. Instead, they turned their passions into professions; it was their purpose.

That thing that nudges you, that you daydream about, that you practice and study, sometimes the thing that gets you in trouble because you're doing that instead of doing what you're supposed to be doing—like homework or cleaning the garage—yeah, *that* thing may be your purpose. You love it, can't imagine life without it, and want to be around others who appreciate it. Now, that doesn't mean everything you love is what you should spend your life doing. We've all met people who love to do stuff the rest of us know they don't do well. They may not even know they don't do it well until they repeatedly get denied the job, don't qualify for the talent show, or fall off the balance beam.

Sure, not everything we enjoy is our purpose, but when considering our purpose, we must not fail to consider our passion.

What Do You Hate?

It may seem logical to consider what you love when weighing purpose, but what you hate? Yes, hate! You ever find yourself enraged about issues, problems, and injustices that make you sick to your stomach, on the verge of upchucking, or even close to telling folks off, but you look around and see that you're the only person with that response? Everyone else is going on about their business, seemingly oblivious or unfeeling. You don't get it, and it ticks you off. Why can't everyone else see what you see or feel what you feel?

Many of us have experienced this, so let's assess. One mistake you may make in a situation like this is concluding that you're overreacting, that whatever it is that raises your blood pressure every time you witness it or think about it is not really a big deal. I mean, if it were something to be up in arms about, everybody would be up in arms with you, right? Instead, it has you up at night while others are sleeping soundly. How does that work? Here's the deal. Others may not react to something you feel strongly about, as obvious as the injustice is, for a very good reason: they're not called to it. We don't all have the same assignment. So we must avoid judging people by our assignment. Your assignment will cause something to rise up within you, a righteous indignation, if you will, at things others don't even notice.

What do you despise? I know of people who rail against child abuse. Now, every single one of us should have an intolerance for child abuse. Not one person with a ticking heart can hear about abuse and not denounce it. But not everyone's response is the same. Some people have a visceral, heart-wrenching response so intense others may look and say, "Get a grip!" But the called have a hatred for the abuse that is so intense they cannot get a grip—meaning they cannot just move on and eat their lunch or watch their television program. They *cannot* get a grip because the injustice has gripped *them*. So do not dismiss what you hate as merely something that rubs you the wrong way. It may be deeper.

The issue is not always as deep as child abuse. Perhaps it's the failure of your local church to make the youth a priority. You notice that much of the ministry is geared toward adults, and there are insufficient, if any, activities for teenagers, who seem to be drifting further and further from the church. Every time the church leadership announces a new outreach, dinner, or program for the twenty-somethings, seniors, or newlyweds, you cringe. You actually get an attitude up in the church! Everyone else is either thrilled, annoyed about another event they have to attend, or not even paying attention, but you're downright upset.

You have a choice to make. You can keep your bad attitude and quit the church because those so-and-so people "don't care anything about my teenagers or me," or you can be part of the solution to a problem you recognize. Why does it seem like no one else notices the teenagers bored at the back of the church? Why don't they care that they are hanging out with the wrong crowd or growing resentful? Doesn't everyone have a working set of eyes like you do? Listen, some people look, but others see. You're going to see things that others do not because of your purpose. Before you march away angry because nobody sees what you see, why don't you get your heart right and consider that your hatred that some are forgotten might be a clue that you're called to bring about the much-needed change? Walking away leaves those young people in the same situation: without help. Taking steps to help may save their lives.

So remember not to ignore what you hate.

What Do Others Say About You?

Throughout our lives, we have heard people advise us to ignore what others say about us. Why? Well, some people like to criticize, and some like to flatter. And I imagine if we had a choice between the two, we'd choose the latter. However, both excessive criticism and flattery can be detrimental to our progress. Each has the capacity to stunt our growth. Criticism often gives us a "woe is me" mentality. You've met those people—the "I can't do anything right," "nothing I say ever makes a difference," "I give up" people. Flattery may give us a big head. "I've got this thing in the bag," we might say. "Nobody can do this better than I can." Then there's the "I'm da man!" delusion. That person is headed for a fall—often because he took to heart the flattery of someone who may have had ulterior motives. I'm not talking about constructive criticism or deserved praise; those are useful to us and can propel us into our purpose. I'm talking about words that tear us down or set us up for failure.

Words from people who have our best interests in mind, however, may be a clue to our purpose. What are others saying about you? From my childhood on up, I heard people say that there was something special about me. I still hear it. I don't say this to brag; I'm just sharing my experiences. As a student, as much of a pain in the neck as I was with my incessant silliness and talking, teachers always told my aunt that I was gifted. In Sunday School and church, my oratorical skills garnered attention. In high school, teachers praised my writing. As a senior taking a creative writing elective, I enjoyed hearing my teacher share my stories with the class. It inspired me to want to improve, to be even better than she said I was. To this day, I do not doubt I have a gift for writing. As a teacher, when my students wrote in class, I often wrote with them and shared my writing as they shared theirs so I could model good writing for them. They would tell me I was a good writer and ask why I hadn't written a book. It confirmed for me what I knew. It gave me more clues to my purpose. So today, I may struggle with my appearance, my cooking ability, even my skills as a driver, but I never struggle with believing I can write well.

In adulthood, I would not be part of any congregation long before someone there recognized the gift in me to speak or teach. They would confirm God's calling upon my life and speak that to me. We want to dismiss such words sometimes because we think that makes us humble or we don't recognize ourselves in the words we hear. But we have to listen as they speak about us—just as we have to listen to that nudge toward what we love and that disgust for what we hate. What others say about us often indicates our purpose.

As a teacher, I know what it is to find that student who stands out. There's just something about him that screams purpose. You probably think that this is the A student, the teacher's pet, the student I call "the look good, smell good" kid, but think again. While I have had "the best and the brightest" fit into that category, more often, students who were royal pains in the rear —some of them failing and misbehaving—had greatness written all over them. My colleagues and I talked about them—the ones we wanted to knock out sometimes. Nonetheless, there was just something about them. It was an honor to tell those students what we recognized in them because we longed so much to see them begin to embrace that truth.

I have stood before audiences of young people and told them that what people say about them is a clue to their purpose. The same is true for adults. We don't stop looking for purpose when we graduate high school. When someone tells you what a great singer you are or that you have leadership skills or you work well with your hands, listen. Sometimes, these words confirm what we've already been feeling, and sometimes, we're hearing something for the first time that we have to mull over. Just be open because what others say about you may be a clue to your purpose in life or the next step in your journey.

CHAPTER 5

USE THE F-WORD

People can be a trip—mean, vindictive, hurtful. And those are just our relatives! It's hard to imagine people can be worse than those family members during Thanksgiving dinner, but believe me, you ain't seen nothing yet. Some people think nothing of lying, cheating, stealing, dragging your name through the mud. That sounds pessimistic, but it's reality. You may not be able to wrap your brain around the idea of someone doing you dirty, but there are people who delight in that stuff. They ain't happy unless you're miserable. They'll turn every good deed you do into something ugly and then convince others to join their smear campaign against you. That's just how some folks flow, so if you're going to succeed in life, you need thick skin. You have to choose your battles wisely. You have to be discerning enough to know when to speak up and when to just let it go. And you're going to have to employ the F-word.

I know: that sounds like good news; you've been itching to throw that F-bomb, and finally, someone is giving you permission to do it! Yes, I am. But it is probably not what you think—and it is most definitely not what you want. Nonetheless, it is what you need.

To reach your full potential, you have to forgive. Oh, I heard what you just thought: "Forgive? That must be a joke 'cause ain't nobody got time for that!" Actually, the reverse is true: "Ain't nobody got time not to forgive." Forgiveness is a key to joy, success, prosperity, and purpose. If you can forgive, you can move ahead. If you cannot forgive, you will never know true freedom. You may look good on the outside. You may even enjoy a measure of success, but you'll be all locked up inside—a slave to bitterness and inner turmoil, which is no way to live.

Consider civil rights leader Medgar Evers, shot in the driveway of his home as he arrived late one night in 1963. The 37-year-old husband and father of three small children lay bleeding. He died in the presence of his family. The murderer, a member of the KKK, was not brought to justice until 1994, 27 years later. The movie *Ghosts of Mississippi* told the story, and I'll never forget what his wife, Myrlie Evers, played by Whoopi Goldberg, said. Asked by her adult children how she could manage not to hate their father's murderer, she quoted her husband: "When you hate, the only one that suffers is you because most of the people you hate don't know it, and the rest don't care." That's the truth—or "troof," as I like to say.

Look, if anyone had a right to be bitter, it would be a woman whose husband was murdered merely because his existence was an affront to those who deemed him unworthy of life. All he wanted was equal rights. This young mom was left a widow, having to raise her children alone, having to pursue justice that seemed more elusive than likely. She could have chosen to be bitter and unforgiving. But her words tell us that she understood that had she harbored unforgiveness, she would have only been heaping further suffering upon herself, and she deserved better.

What about you? What do you deserve? You may have a good reason to be upset. You may be justified in holding a grudge. But who really suffers?

Have you ever run into someone you can't stand? As soon as you see him, you get that sickening knot in your stomach, your whole mood changes, and you scowl. You try not to pay attention to this person who is a short distance away, but you can't help yourself. You find yourself glancing repeatedly and, you think, inconspicuously. Instead of seeing someone equally disturbed, you see someone who is happy, free, and without a care. This only serves to make you even more bitter.

This is the point Myrlie was making: most of the people you've allowed to steal your peace are oblivious to your grudge, and the others simply don't give a flying fig. So why, after you've been done wrong by someone else, would you do yourself wrong, too? Forgive.

Why Don't We Forgive?

There are several reasons we don't forgive.

I'm Right

When we feel our cause is right, it's difficult to abandon it. We're right. They're wrong. Isn't that reason enough to harbor unforgiveness? Well, that depends. Do you want to be right, or do you want to be free to move on and be your best self? Your answer will determine your course of action. Jails are full of folks who are right. How many times have we heard about people who spent decades incarcerated, only for evidence to surface that they did nothing wrong? They were right all along when they declared their innocence. That wasn't enough to set them free, however. You can be right but locked up, just as you can be wrong but sincere. You hear people say, "Bless his heart. He's so sincere." Well, that's great. There's nothing like sincerity, but just because you sincerely believe something doesn't make it correct. And being right when you say you were done dirty doesn't change your circumstance. To be free to forgive, you have to come to grips with the truth that—right or wrong—the situation is what it is, and you're the one suffering when you hold on to anger and bitterness.

This takes us back to Cherie's cry to her mother: "But Mommy, I can't want to." That's how we are when it comes to releasing those who have wronged us. We don't always remain bitter because we believe we should. Sometimes, we know good and well we should let it go, but we can't want to. I've been there. I have had to cry out to God and say, "Lord, I don't want to forgive. I don't even feel like praying for You to help me forgive. But I'm asking You to help me anyway." I've even gone on to tell the Lord all about it. Some say, "You mean you tell the Lord how angry you are and what you think of the person?" Why not? Here's how I look at it: He knows anyway, so I might as well be real. I'm not fooling Him, and, truth be told, I'm probably not fooling anyone else, either. When bitterness settles inside our hearts, it has a way of manifesting on the outside.

Here's my advice: forgive, and do it quickly. The best example I have of that is Jesus on the cross. He prayed a prayer that is the ultimate depiction of grace and love. "Father, forgive them, for they know not what they do." Why is this so powerful? Look, it's hard enough to forgive someone who asks for it. It's extra hard to forgive when the wrong-doers have not even acknowledged that they have done wrong, much less apologized.

Let it go fast because the longer you hold onto it, the more deeply embedded in your spirit it becomes, the angrier you become, and the more difficult it becomes to get past. Holding on to unforgiveness is punishing yourself. Remember that "most of the people you hate don't know it, and the rest don't care." So why let them win? Do not let being right imprison you. It's better to be free.

I Can't Forget

Some won't forgive because they cannot forget the wrong done to them. But who said anything about forgetting? Yeah, I know. We've heard it all of our lives: "Forgive and forget." I prefer to employ what the character Madea in a Tyler Perry movie said when addressing someone who found it difficult to forgive: "Don't forgive and forget. Forgive—and remember!" Forgetting may seem impossible, so don't worry about that. Madea was saying you had better remember so you don't find yourself in that situation again. Forgive

PUSH YOUR WAY TO PURPOSE

and remember! Having said that, I do believe that at times, "memory loss" is a blessing that gets us through pain. Sometimes, it's the result of a supernatural healing. Nonetheless, just because you remember something someone did to you doesn't mean you have unforgiveness in your heart. Remembering it sheds light sometimes, brings much-needed lessons, and enables us to share wisdom with others. So whether you forgive and forget or forgive and remember, the key is to forgive.

I Fail to Recognize My Need of Forgiveness

Here's an activity. Take out a sheet of paper. On one side, list the people you need to forgive and what they did. On the other side, write down the things you have done wrong and to whom. Afterwards, compare the lists. I did this activity once when I was conducting jail ministry. I knew the women inmates were dealing with various issues. Many of them had been hurt out there in the streets. Men had disappointed them, friends had turned on them, and childhood innocence had been stolen from them. They were carrying the weight of abuse and heartache, with valid reasons to be angry in some cases. The writing, however, served as a visual. They discovered as they began to think, write, and then compare both lists that they had given others just as much reason to need to forgive them as others had given them to forgive the wrongdoing perpetrated against them.

We often think of prisoners as simply inmates. What many of them were, however, were moms suffering from knowing that because of their choices, they could not be there for their children. Some also lamented worrying their parents with their lifestyles and by their incarceration. Guilt engulfed them.

When people think of jail, they don't imagine women who are soft-hearted and loving, susceptible to tears in an instant. But many of these women were just that. In fact, I rarely encountered women there who were hardened criminals. I met many a repeat offender, though. I'd see many of the ladies again and again. They'd get arrested, come to the jail ministry and get right with God, eventually get released, and return. They had not learned how to be free on the outside.

Their list opened their eyes to seeing that we have all done wrong. We have all hurt people, even those most precious to us. We can all name an area in which we'd love to get a redo. We all need forgiveness sometimes. Taking time to be honest with ourselves makes it easier to forgive other people, which takes me to my next point.

I Can't Forgive Myself

People who cannot forgive themselves have the hardest time forgiving others. They are some of the most critical people you'll ever meet. You don't want to work for one of these people, and you sure don't want to marry one. If folks don't show *themselves* mercy, you know they won't show you any. You don't stand a chance.

We have all met people like this. They can't see past the last mistake someone made, and they're quick to remind you of yours. They throw your mess-ups in your face and wield it as a weapon against you. They pat themselves on the back and stab you in yours.

We tend to see these people as having it all together. They come across as above the fray of imperfection. Because they have it all together, how could they ever have patience for our frailty? This is usually the narrative they've written themselves, one that is far from the truth. In reality, many of them are not confident and self-assured, instead lacking in self-esteem and looking for the approval of others. They don't withhold forgiveness from others because they believe others don't deserve it—not really. They withhold forgiveness from others because they withhold it from themselves, and they withhold it from themselves because they don't believe they deserve it.

Insecurity makes strange characters out of people. When we give in to it, instead of seeing ourselves as fallible and in need of grace and mercy, we see ourselves as failures, and to disguise it, we come down hard on others. We cannot tolerate their weaknesses because that would force us to acknowledge our own. So we seek to rid our consciousness of those weaknesses by castigating those who exhibit it.

The ability to forgive others is tied to our ability to forgive ourselves, which is linked to giving ourselves permission to just be human.

Forgive others. They're worth it. Forgive yourself. You're worth it, too.

CHAPTER 6

TOOLBOX FOR SUCCESS

Every mechanic carries a toolbox. He stacks it with things he will need to do the job he's been hired to do. Without it, he is basically useless. Repairmen are in the same boat. If they show up to do a job and realize they left the toolbox at the office, they've just lost out on that job and have probably made a few people upset in the process. Every job has its toolbox. It may not have a hammer, screwdriver, and nails, but it has the tools necessary to complete the task successfully.

I started several school years playing a game with my students that emphasized this. We all gathered in a large circle, and students would have to call a classmate's name and toss him the ball, underhanded. The classmate would catch it—hopefully—and then call a name and throw the ball to that person. Students were told before the game began that they had to remember from whom they got the ball and to whom they tossed it.

After everyone had received the ball once, that part of the game was over, and I would inform them that we were doing it again, in the same order. That, of course, evoked a plethora of hemming and hawing. They wanted to play again, but they had forgotten the guideline to pay attention to the pesky detail of the order of tosses. Nonetheless, we somehow managed to find our way through. As far as they were concerned, it was just a fun game—and a bit chaotic, which, of course, to seventh-graders means the same thing. The crazier the game, the more fun for them.

After we had played this a few times, aiming for a flawless round (which inevitably took a while because every time we messed up, I made us start again), I would inform them that we were going to do it again, but this time, we were going backwards. "Say what?!" I would hear, as students soaked in the added chaos—and loved every minute of it.

There was more up my sleeve. After a few rounds of the backwards round, I would go behind my desk and produce another ball I had hidden. The second ball would be of a different color. Students' eyes would bug out. Then I would announce, holding up one ball, "This ball will go forward." Then holding the other, I would say, "And this one will go backwards— simultaneously." I would tell them that one person was not to end up with both balls at one time. All the rules that were previously in effect remained, but the added craziness made them difficult to remember, so students would forget to call the name first, throw the ball underhanded, on and on. Before long, somebody would get knocked in the neck with the ball, hit the light fixture above, forget the throwing order, or some other such mayhem.

When students returned to their seats, we would debrief. My question: "What was required to be successful in this task?" More often than not, we had not been successful, but hey!

The best learning is learning that takes place without realizing you're learning, so it was always a joy to see students' faces change from the faces of those just playing a game—or so they thought—to processing what had taken place.

As they contemplated my question and began to share their thoughts, I recorded what they said on the board for all to see. They realized just how much was required to play our little game. Some of the responses were: rules, cooperation, communication, collaboration, a leader, participants, skills, a location, and yes, tools. I would then tell my students that these same things would be necessary for success in our school year together.

Let's park at tools. We could have a place to play, people to participate, ability to communicate, skills to throw and catch, rules to guide us, and a leader to enforce them, but without the tools—the balls—we'd be standing around in a circle staring at one another.

Every successful endeavor requires tools. I carry a toolkit with me sometimes when I deliver a motivational address. Let's unpack it now, see what's in it, and discover how they help us succeed. We'll also take a look at the obstacles that impede the effectiveness of those tools.

Seeds

Farmers and gardeners plant seeds, water them, and wait. They do it not because they see the fully grown vegetables. They do it because they *want* to see them.

They take action by faith. Faith motivates them. By faith, they work the ground long before they plant the seeds. Faith makes them tend to that ground. Faith keeps them from uprooting what they've planted when they don't see the end result right away. Faith says that if they just do their part and wait, they will reap what they have sown, and they will reap much more than they have sown.

This corresponds with the necessity of faith in our lives. We have to have that packet of seeds. Seeds remind us that no matter what it looks like, no matter how small what we have at our disposal appears to be, no matter how unfruitful the ground seems, we have to see the end result, and since it hasn't occurred yet, the only way to see it is by faith. Faith gives us a picture of what we're shooting for, which keeps us moving forward.

What is it you desire? Wishing for it isn't good enough. The farmer can wish all day long for a harvest. But faith is not a wish. Faith moves him beyond wishing and makes him believe that it can happen, which makes him do his part.

But faith has obstacles, and its biggest obstacle is fear. Fear works against faith, rendering it impotent and paralyzing us in the process. All kinds of fears exist.

Fear of heights is called acrophobia.

Fear of confined places is called claustrophobia.

Arachnophobia is the fear of spiders.

Ergophobia is the fear of work.

There is no end to the various phobias people face. Believe it or not, there's even a fear of fear; it's aptly called phobophobia.

Faith demands action. Fear causes inaction. So fear is the enemy of faith.

During the start of a new athletics season at school, I would ask students if they tried out for a particular sport. Always, someone would tell me she had not, and when I asked why, she would answer, "Because I was afraid I wouldn't make the team." This is how irrational fear is. Here was someone who said she was afraid she wouldn't make the team, so she didn't try out. Not trying out meant she was definitely not going to make the team. By not trying out, she guaranteed that what she feared would happen actually happened: she wouldn't be on the team. She would rather do nothing at all than do everything possible. Fear kills the faith tool.

Scissors

Scissors are another necessary tool of success. We use them to cut some folks off. No, I did not say use them to cut folks up! I said to cut them off. There's a distinct—life-saving—difference. Cut them off, but don't cut them! (See chapter on forgiveness!)

We allow people into our circle who are not good for us. They are toxic, and we would be better served if we let them go. As I tell audiences, some people remain in our lives whether we like it or not. Teenagers cannot cut off their parents or siblings, for example. However, as they come into their own and recognize their worth, they can choose the influence they will allow them to have in their lives. Some parents are wonderful and daily reinforce their children's worth. If the world had more of these, more children would grow up feeling loved, confident, and secure. Let's face it, though. Too many children are not growing up with that kind of reinforcement. Some people are parents simply because they gave birth, but they do not have a parenting instinct anywhere in them. There may come a time when the child recognizes the negativity and cuts it off. But that can only be done once that child recognizes that he or she deserves better.

When we spend too much time with people who are not good for us, it impacts us. It's impossible for it not to. It's like being in a room with a skunk. Plug your nose, close your eyes, clog your ears, but after a while, you're going to stink. There's no wishing the funk away, praying the funk away, or talking the funk away. The only answer is to get the funk away. In other words, you walk away. Cut the skunk out of your life. Everyone needs a good pair of scissors for these situations.

You'd be surprised how much more you can accomplish when you surround yourself with the right people at the right time. I often allowed students to choose their own groups for the first group project of the school year. After a couple weeks of collaboration, completing the project, and presenting it to the class, we would sit around to self-evaluate. Many times, I heard students say they would prefer that I select the groups next time. That was always interesting because these were the same people who had begged to pick their groups. Why? So they could work with their friends, of course. Experience taught them, however, that when they picked their groups, they picked their friends, people who were fun to talk to and who made them laugh but not necessarily people with whom they could produce their best work. This is not to say that they were bad people, but they were simply not the best people to work with. After trying to work together, students realized, "Hey, this didn't work out right. I need to cut this person off for now so I can be my best self. We can catch up and play around some other time."

Of course, there are people who are bad news, too, and we need to be mindful of them. They are bad influences on us. You ever notice that certain people bring out the worst in you? Pull out those scissors and cut them off. This may have to be a long-term cutoff. Do what's necessary for your own growth.

Ring

Have you ever been to a wedding? One of the most precious parts of the ceremony is the exchanging of the rings. "With this ring, I thee wed as a token of my love," the couples say to one another. The ring is a circle—unbroken—which symbolizes a love that is eternal. It represents a covenant.

The ring is as vital a tool as the scissors. Just as you must cut off those who need to be cut off, you need to stick closely to those who enhance you. You need people who lift you up and encourage you. Understand that these are not people who tickle your ears all the time. They do not always say what you want to hear, but they do tell you what you need to hear.

Human nature is to keep "yes people" nearby. "Yes people" agree with you and validate your feelings, no matter how ridiculous they are. When you're angry and ready to tell someone off, "yes people" say, "Girl, I hear you. You need to put her in her place! Who does she think she is?" We like to hear that. It means we're right, and who doesn't want to be right? But we need some folks in our lives who look us straight in the eyes and say, "You know what? Just stop. You're dead wrong. Your attitude is stinking up the place, and you need to cut it out." That won't make you feel good, but it will help you mature. That's what a real relationship provides. That's what a covenant does.

Covenant relationships aren't just good for putting you in your place. They involve giving positive feedback and support also. It's the whole ball of wax. The full circle. The ring, if you will.

When people have wounded us, we allow those scars to lie to us and tell us that we don't need anybody. We can go it alone. We got it in the bag. The truth is we've got nothing in the bag—not alone. We need one another if we are going to succeed. The Bible says, "Two are better than one." It's true. This doesn't mean we don't have moments of walking alone. That, too, is one of life's realities, but those should be the exceptions to life's rules, not the pattern by which we live out our days.

Eyeglasses

Eyeglasses represent vision. We cannot move from Point A to Point B unless we see what's in front of us. People who wear prescription lenses reach for them the first thing in the morning. Before getting out of bed, they reach over to the nightstand and feel around for those spectacles. They rely on them to go about their day. They're useless without them. Those who wear contact lenses put the glasses on until they get the contacts in; that's how much they need to be able to see. We, too, need corrective lenses so we can focus accurately on what matters and see things clearly.

Have you ever been a passenger in a car when the driver saw something that grabbed his attention? He focused in on it, and the next thing you knew, the car was headed in that direction. It can be a frightening experience when you realize that you're headed to the left, toward the beautiful Christmas lights the driver pointed out, and the road doesn't curve in that direction! It's also frightening when we take our eyes off what matters and focus on other things, some of which look appealing—bright, shiny, entertaining. But sometimes, it's just a trap to sidetrack us. Since we tend to go in the direction we look, we need to look in the right direction, and we need to see the path clearly. We must have a good pair of glasses to help us do that.

When my glasses are on, I assess situations better. Thus, I make better decisions. I am more likely, therefore, to arrive where I want to go than to get lost —or worse, to crash and self-destruct. Each one of us desires to arrive at our destiny. We want to fulfill our purpose, so we need eyeglasses that help us see clearly.

Shovel

The shovel comes in handy to bury the past. Dig the hole wide and deep, and dump in the past. Dump in the things you wish you could change but cannot. Dump in the mistakes you've made along the way. Even dump in successes that you've been leaning on. I probably lost you with the last one. Who wants to bury success? Okay, maybe you don't want to completely bury those successes, but dump your inclination to refer to them incessantly as if your greatest accomplishments are behind you. They're not. They're ahead of you. If you find that you're always reflecting wistfully on some great past moment when you should be living in the present, that needs to change. It's robbing your potential. Bury that thief.

The shovel is also the tool to do what we discussed earlier: forgive. Just let it go. Release. Bury animosity toward others, and bury animosity toward yourself. Keep that shovel handy, and use it early and often.

Fatigues

There is hardly a more fitting example of strength, courage, and perseverance than a member of the United States military. That's why I've chosen fatigues as the last tool in the toolbox, to represent these heroic men and women. Soldiers understand the cost of victory. They know that it requires training, teamwork, and sacrifice. Quitting is not an option, so preparation is necessary. Trusting their fellow soldiers is not a suggestion; it's the difference between life and death. Having their own agenda is antithetical to the mission, so they lay it down. And if the mission demands it, they are committed to laying down their lives also. Soldiers are in for the duration—all-in. They must, therefore, dress for the task. Their uniform indicates that they represent something greater than self. It serves a purpose. It's not about personal taste or fashion. It shows they are enlisted to serve and that they have submitted to that enlistment. U.S. soldiers are the world's finest. They're hardcore. They will not melt under pressure. They never give up.

Success always comes at a price. To live up to our potential, we have to be like that soldier in those fatigues. We, too, must clothe ourselves in our true identity, an identity where compromise is never considered, quitting is a foreign word, and failure is not an option. We must recognize that there are enemies all around us and booby traps to ensnare us. Minefields are waiting to blow up the possibilities that invite us. But there's a fighting spirit within us and a camaraderie with others that fortify us. I know we'd all prefer easy over difficult, but that simply isn't the way it goes down most of the time, so in times of peace, we have to determine that when all hell breaks out, we won't. We'll stay in the fight, hold tight, and win.

CHAPTER 7
LESSONS FROM THE SIDELINE:
IT'S HARD

Who goes into a situation hoping it will be difficult and take us to the limit? We would call that insane. We look for easy. We go about trying to find ways to lighten the load, lessen the stress, and eliminate the mess. We've been trained to go about our business in that way. It makes sense, doesn't it?

It makes perfect sense for mediocre people. But you're not mediocre. I know that because you're reading this book. You don't continue to read a book like this if you just want to go with the flow, to go along to get along. You may not even pick it up to begin with after glancing at the title. So you want more. And because you do, you are not afforded what those who are content with the status quo are. You don't get to take the easy road. You actually must seek out the hard.

I had a personal trainer who would always say to me, "Remember, you're trying to make it harder, not easier." The first time I heard Sergio say that, it blew me away. It went against lifelong conditioning that said, "Work smarter, not harder." It seemed to me that my ultimate goal in anything, including those workout sessions that took me to the max, was to make things easier. Positioning myself to feel the burn hotter or make the lift tougher did not come naturally to me. But he would say it often. Actually, he would start the sentence, and I was expected to complete it. He'd say, "Remember, you always want to make it..." And I was supposed to finish the sentence with "harder," though everything in me said, "The devil is a liar! I do not want to make it harder!"

But when I reflect on the years prior to hearing Sergio say those words, I can find the same mindset in my coaching style. I was obsessed with the little things —the hard little things or the little hard things or however one wants to look at it. I subscribed to the idea that "if you take care of the little things, the big things will take care of themselves." Not everyone understood that, but I insisted. If the team was running sprints baseline to baseline, I expected my players' toes to touch the line—not an inch to the baseline, but to actually touch the baseline. If players were running suicides, which are back-and-forth sprints that require touching the floor with the hand, I expected them to touch the floor with their hands— not lean down and wave at the floor, missing it, but touch the floor.

Some wonder what difference it makes. It makes all the difference. It's about mindset. It's about commitment. Losers question what difference it makes. To winners, it's obvious. Winners embrace a spirit of excellence. It becomes a part of them. They take care of the little things, such as bending a fraction of an inch more—which requires extra effort and makes the exercise harder—and the big things take care of themselves.

One of the most painful drills in basketball is the defensive slide. Participants must get down low, similar to a sitting position, and slide around the gym, palms up, legs remaining the same distance apart, feet never meeting or crossing. Trust me: it ain't easy. It hurts like Hades, in fact. Legs begin to burn quickly. It hurts even when players aren't doing it at 100 percent, when they don't get down as low as they should, so you can only imagine the pain when they do it properly. It takes a lot to stay down low. Sweat pops out on foreheads. Players moan in agony. Legs tremble.

Is the purpose just to torment players? Of course not. It's to prepare them to do what it takes to win: play defense. As I've said, if defense doesn't hurt, you're not doing it right. "Coach, it hurts!" Of course, it hurts. It's supposed to hurt. I believed then and still believe now that you can take two evenly matched teams, two equally talented teams, and when it comes down to the nitty-gritty, the team that prepared better wins. Winning doesn't just happen. Winning requires preparation. The one who comes out on top is the one who touched the floor on those suicides, the one whose toes touched the line on those sprints, the one who sat low in that defensive slide. That one prepared and conditioned for victory—above and beyond. That one was willing to hurt to get there. I told my team we would be the better-prepared team on the floor. That was my goal. At the end of my coaching career, my team was the superior team on the court in most scenarios, but even if we had not been, I was determined that we would be the better-prepared, the better-conditioned. We practiced that way. Our success was not accidental; it was by design. My last two seasons coaching included practicing six days a week. While other teams were sleeping on Saturdays, I imagine, the Hudson Bluehawks team was in the gym at 8 a.m. Did I want to get up early every Saturday? Definitely not. I mean, I got up early every weekday for work and every Sunday for church. Sleeping a little late on Saturdays would have been Heaven. But losing is hell, and we wanted no part of it. My girls, their parents, and our community knew we had a nucleus who could win our conference championship, and they expected it. So to practice we went. Those last two years, we won the Patroon Conference championship, something no other girls' basketball team had done in the history of our school. I say all this not to brag on my players, and certainly not to brag on myself, but to illustrate that it was a commitment to do it hard that made our winning look easy to those on the outside—many of whom were probably asleep on Saturdays while we were in the gym.

I Hate That I Need You

You know what else is hard? Relying on other people. Few things in life lead to more frustration. I've already written that we need to be in covenant relationships with people, but did I mention the obvious? It ain't easy. In fact, it's downright hard. Talk to any couple about marriage, and within minutes of the conversation, you'll hear, "It's hard." I'm talking about happily married couples. Don't even get me started on bad marriages. My response to the pronouncement that marriage is hard was to think, "Man, who's got time for that? Does it ever get easy?"

Even apart from the marriage relationship, relationships in general are hard. When you enter one, you're saying, "Bring on the hard." You ever notice that people who have been hurt often retreat and try to go it alone? It's too hard to trust again, too risky. Yes, it's both of those things.

I held my players to a high standard off and on the court. This included what they wore on the bus, what time they showed up to home games, what time they went to the locker room during the junior varsity game as they prepared to take the court for their varsity contest. Violating the rules had consequences.

One thing I was adamant about was showing up to practice on time. It's easy to think that you live unto yourself, that failing to give your all affects only you, but that's a lie. It affects everyone who needs you. Your team needs you—and your team is not just a basketball team. For you, it may be your family, your co-workers, your drill team, and more. Your presence or absence affects more than you, therefore.

I remember the Saturday morning practice when two players came in late. In one practice, the whole team had to run because of a player's tardiness. That was hard—and some might say harsh—but people can understand that better than what I did on this Saturday.

I told the latecomers to sit down and relax while the rest of the team ran. It was my way of showing them that their actions mattered. It was also my understanding of human nature kicking in. See, peer pressure is more effective than pressure from a coach. Teammates may have a lot of mercy on one another, but they're not God: their mercy doesn't endure forever. When people bust their tails and have to cover yours, too, their mercy reaches its end rather soon. So there were a couple of methods to my madness.

It was hard for the girls who were running, but it was harder for the girls who were sitting. They tried to resist, to insist they should be doing the running. My answer? "No. You sit down. Your teammates will run for you." Some say I was wrong. I don't know if wrong or right figures into it. I do know that it was hard— hard all the way around. But I also believed that it was a necessary life-lesson. Teammates, whether literal or figurative, need one another. If one is lax, the whole group pays the price, just as the one who soars often carries the others on her back, making everyone better, making the team—the marriage, the workplace, the choir—function better. I'd love to think I can do it all alone. I hate that it's true, but it is: I need certain people. It's hard to be vulnerable like that, but it's necessary.

As unbending as my coaching approach usually was, I cared about my players, and they knew that. I recall the tough decision I had to make in my last season when we were undefeated both in and out of our conference and had a great opportunity to go far in sectionals and make more history. The regular season ended, and we were in the postseason. My star player missed our Saturday morning practice. I received no call, no anything. At that practice, I could hear the buzz from players because they knew exactly what that meant. We were going into this win-or-go-home game without our leading scorer and intense defender. We had a talented team all around, but you just couldn't replace this player. But my rules were clear: if you didn't show up and didn't notify me, you didn't play in the next game. The tension was palpable. This time, the team wouldn't have minded a teammate coming late and having to run for her while she sat, but it was not in the cards. Practice ended—and still no star player.

I believe in follow-through. You don't make rules to break them, despite the adage to the contrary. You also have to abide by principles. Some things are more important than winning, aren't they?

Our next practice brought an intense discussion with my assistant coach about how to handle this. I had spoken to the player, who was apologetic and also quite nervous about how this would unfold. I had a hard decision to make. I had players there who had worked their behinds off all season, many of them even before the season, to prepare for this year. Some were seniors, including this particular player. They had practiced six days a week, and they were undefeated. This was the year to get it done. We had already won the conference title for the second consecutive year, but this team was hungry for more, and they had worked so hard for it. We were about to face teams that were equally talented, at least, teams we had never faced before and didn't know anything about, except what was on paper. This was not the time to mess with what had gotten us to this point. But her behavior had tied my hands, and I didn't appreciate it. We coaches were there at that previous practice, and the rest of the team was there at that practice, but her absence put us in a bad position. I cared a lot about this player, as I did about all of my players, but this one was extra special. I had coached her the longest. I took her on the varsity team as a middle schooler, whereas most don't get to play varsity ball until eleventh grade.

There was no way to enforce the rule without disrupting the team and hurting our chances. My assistant coach, Kristen Fonda, and I consulted about it as the team captains led the drills. From my perspective, I had two options: one was to sit her out the entire game and hope for the best for our team, and the other was to let her play for the sake of the team. This is the epitome of hard. I guess she had gotten a memo from Sergio telling her to make coaching harder, not easier.

Fonda, as I called my assistant, was much more lenient by nature than I was—the players all loved her —and she was in favor of option two. It was a moral dilemma for me. After all, I'm the teacher who complained that students who weren't showing up as they should weren't learning the right values if they managed to pass the class anyway. When my administrator asked, "Are you trying to teach your students morals, or are you teaching literature?" I answered, "Well, I hope I'm teaching morals and using literature to do it." That's what you're dealing with when you get me. So what would it look like if I put winning above honoring my word and if I sold out the standards I established—standards I wanted to be life-lessons I modeled for my girls? But after much contemplation and consultation with my assistant, I came to the conclusion that in this case, honoring my rule to discipline that one player was not as important as honoring the sacrifice and hard work of all of my players.

In a private conversation, I scolded her and let her know how disappointed I was. I told her she had put me in an extremely tough position and had also let her teammates down, that her actions were selfish. I still remember her saying, "Don't you think this matters to me, too?" She was drawing my attention to her hard work all season and saying she wanted to win as much as everyone else. I had no doubt that was true. She practiced hard and played hard, and we would not have had the success we had without her. She was an athlete to the core, and she gave me more moments of joy as a coach than I can count, but that doesn't change the fact that throughout the years, she also gave me a few gray hairs, and this was one of those moments.

In that private conversation, I was vocal about where I stood. I told her that against my conscience, I was going to do what was best for the team. I was going to allow her to play—not for her, but for our team. I had to live with myself for selling out my guidelines, yes, but I realized I could find a way to live with that, but I could not live with making everyone else suffer for her infraction. In this case, the right thing was doing the wrong thing, according to the rules. It was hard to break my rules, but easy was simply not an option I could stomach.

When I broke the news to the team, no one expressed disappointment in my decision to let her play. Rather, the only thing I sensed was relief. They were elated that I would allow her to play, and their faith in accomplishing their goals skyrocketed.

We absolutely have to take what we do seriously. Otherwise, we will behave as if what we do isn't significant. My first year as a coach was probably my most frustrating. Players who had played under the previous coach had to adjust to my style, and that wasn't easy. It was a rebuilding year at that, which always brings its own set of challenges. I had younger players also, and they were being asked to step up and produce results. And let's not forget this was a girls' team, and anyone who has ever had to coach, teach, parent—or anything—girls knows how difficult that can be. We ladies are a trip! So we were not short on drama and personal conflicts, either.

After a rough start, I decided it was time to have a tough-love conversation with the team. One of my younger players said during that talk, "It's just a game." Wrong thing to say to this coach. In fact, it was one of the worst things anyone could say to me—and you better believe she never said it again. I did not expect everyone to be as passionate about basketball as I was, but I did expect that when they stepped on the court, it appeared as if they were. Their passion may not have been at my personal level, but they were going to have to fool me somehow.

"A game?" I said. "If you want to play a game, you go play Checkers. This is basketball!" No offense to Checkers lovers everywhere, but that's how I felt: basketball and Checkers don't belong in the same sentence. What we were doing mattered, and if we were going to do it, we were going to do it well and with everything we had, even in the hard moments— probably especially in the hard moments. This is how we are to approach life.

Life presents us with all kinds of hard decisions, and usually, there's a lot more on the line than a basketball game. Some decisions are about how to care for a sick loved one, the best approach to confronting a cheating partner, or when to take the plunge into self-employment. They involve relying not just on ourselves, but on others who may or may not live up to the challenge. Decide now that you are going to face those hard things. You're not going to go the easy route. It's not an option. You're going to dig deep, suck it up, and come out on top.

CHAPTER 8

RAISE YOUR EXPECTATIONS

"Whether you believe you can or whether you believe you can't, you're right." I heard this a long time ago, and it has stuck with me. It behooves you to believe you can. For those who always have high expectations, that's easy. But most people struggle with believing that they can accomplish more, enjoy greater success, or even just be happy. So it's time to raise those expectations. Those who are full of confidence and have won at the highest level, guess what: you're still here, which means you're not done. Your influence has not reached its max. So you must raise your expectations also so that you leave no path untouched that your fingerprints are meant to mark. The bottom line is that none of us has an excuse—not the underachievers and not the extraordinary. Each of us must reach higher. How do we do that? We start by raising our expectations. Remember, what you believe about yourself is your reality.

I've heard that if your vision is within reach, it's too small. We need a vision that shows us something we do not currently possess—one that requires not just hard work, but hardcore faith. This chapter will deal with four requirements to raising expectations. The first three are all centered around belief.

Believe in the Mission

If you don't believe in the mission, you won't give yourself to it. You'll focus on something more important to you at the moment. How many things have we started that we have not finished? We discussed this earlier. Some of the unfinished business stems from a lack of focus, but often, it's a lack of believing in the mission, believing that it matters. When the mission is worthwhile to you, it's easier to give yourself to it. When it's not, it's just more work.

I knew the first day I ever stood in front of a group that God had given me the gift of communication. I'm not just talking about being able to put sentences together. It was more than that. It was the ability to open my mouth and command attention. I didn't demand it. I just opened my mouth. That started at a young age because I was forced to do it even when I did not want to. It soon became something cherished rather than a chore. When I submitted to what was obviously the plan for my life—teaching—I knew also that I was called to teach. I always knew that I would not retire from teaching, that God would change my assignment at some point, but I knew I would always be a teacher, even if not in a school classroom. Classroom teaching is both rewarding and frustrating. Toward the end of my career, as I got closer to resigning, it became even more frustrating. I lost some of the passion I had enjoyed. It was still there, but the red tape, the resistance, and the change in culture, among other irritants, had ebbed away at that passion. Never, however, did I doubt that what I had done throughout the years was worthwhile. I knew it was, and if I ever doubted it, former students and former colleagues were sure to let me know.

I no longer stand in front of a class and read literature to my students in the various accents of characters or try to impress upon them the power of an expanding vocabulary or bang my head against the board while begging them—again—to start a sentence with a capital letter. However, I sometimes have the honor of going to schools and talking to students, trying to inspire them. The passion is still there. Every seed planted into the soil of their lives is worthwhile. It's a mission field that is ripe for the picking. I believe that, and because I do, I can raise my expectations at every opportunity to be a voice and to have an influence. Each time gets better. More lives are touched. More hope is spread. More. More. More.

Just as I believed in the mission as a classroom teacher, I believed in the mission to leave teaching. I always knew it was coming, but when it did, it was unnerving. How does one walk away after 17-plus years? It was the only profession I had ever known. It was what I did well. And I was going to leave and then do…what? I didn't even have a job waiting when I resigned. Understand when I say I never recommend that. You've heard it before: "Never quit one job until you get another." But for me, after a friend encouraged me to trust God and move forward, sparking tears I never expected, I took steps to see what this crazy idea was all about. I chose to go against my belief about quitting without having something else waiting because I knew it was right— for me, for that time, for my purpose. Just as I had obeyed the call to teach, I wanted to obey the call to leave teaching. After much prayer, discussion, and counseling with my pastors, I took that leap of faith. I didn't know at the time what would come of it, but I knew it was the right thing to do. I knew God had something waiting for me that I wouldn't receive if I didn't let go of what I already had. It's like opening up your closed fist, releasing what's in your hand so that He can put more into it. For me, it was more than a change of profession; it was also a change of location. And fast. I made my decision in August to resign from teaching, informed my employer in September, had my last day in mid-October, and on the first day of November, I was on the road, driving to Missouri to live. What a turnaround! As I made that 19-hour drive, no one was with me. They couldn't have fit in the car anyway! The car was packed so high that I could barely see out of the windows. I left all I knew in New York and set out on this new journey because I believed what was ahead of me was greater than what was behind me. I believed in the mission. The mission I already had was rather good, but I'm learning that when the situation calls for it and when the time is right, we have to relinquish the good thing for the God-thing. It requires serious courage, and we'll never do it if we don't believe, so believe in the mission.

Believe in Yourself

Okay, so now you believe in the mission. It's there. You see it. And you believe it's a God-thing—for someone else! Sound familiar? Look, if you are to raise your expectations, you can't just believe in the mission. You have to believe that you can master that mission. You have to see yourself in the midst of it.

Often, we find ourselves saying things like, "I'm nobody," mistakenly believing that this makes us humble. It doesn't. It makes us liars. Imagine what it would be like for someone to build a luxurious mansion, taking great care with every brick laid, every room crafted. Nothing was spared. It was the best of the best. Upon completion, people spoke of its beauty, its purpose, its creator even. The gorgeous mansion, however, magically empowered to speak, repeatedly said, "I'm just a shack." First, this is a lie. To everyone with clear vision, it's obviously not a shack. But even more important, it's an insult to the builder. The builder gave us his best work, a masterpiece and a work of art. To respond by saying it is a shack demeans both the creator and his creation.

We are like that building. We have been created in the image of God. We were hand-designed and fashioned as He wanted us. In other words, we are special. To say otherwise is both a lie and an insult, and it's obvious to everyone who can see. This is key. Life, with all its hurdles and hurts, often obscures our vision. We need that vision restored by the truth, and we must be willing to respond to that truth. My friend Kia expressed this to me once. She said, "I've come to realize that I am all that!" This declaration sounds delusional at worst, narcissistic at best. It's neither. She had the revelation we all need: not acknowledging our value and potential is not humility; it's foolishness. It's also a choice. I can choose not to embrace this truth. I can choose to live subpar or mediocre, or I can choose to go farther, reach higher, achieve greater. I can choose to believe in myself. If I am to raise my expectations, which is necessary to live out my purpose, I must make that choice.

Take my cat, Trooper, as an example. I started noticing that Trooper would stand by the door that leads to where I keep his water, food, and litter box. It was usually wide open, but every once in a while, I would have it only partway open. It was certainly wide enough for Trooper to walk through, so when he would stand there and meow to get my attention, I was lost. "Trooper, just go through the door," I would say. He wouldn't. He'd just give me that look that comes naturally to him, the look that says, "Hey, human, you're here to serve, so get to it! Open the door." I would shake my head, open the door wide, and he would walk through. He could have easily fit all along, so he didn't need my help at all, but he thought he did, so I was an obedient lackey and played doorman.

After asking countless times, "Trooper, why won't you just go through the door?" and getting no response from my little guy, I just figured it is what it is and did what I was called upon to do. It is, after all, the life of every cat's parent: just do what you're told, human, and no one gets hurt!

But one day, as Trooper stood at the half-opened, plenty-big-enough-for-him-to-walk-through door, it hit me. Boom! Revelation! Trooper didn't go through the door because he didn't believe he could fit through it. Okay, that part was obvious. But the question is, "Why didn't he believe he could fit through the door?" And the answer is this: I could see Trooper's size and the size of the door crack for what they were; thus, I could easily assess that he was small enough to fit, but in Trooper's mind, he was much bigger than what I saw. In Trooper's mind, he was so big, in fact, there was no way he could fit through the door. He may have been cat-sized to everyone else, but to him, he was the size of a lion, and, indeed, he had the spirit of a lion. He must have been thinking, "I cannot fit through this crack. I am much too big for this!"

This is what we humans are missing. We fail to understand that we are too big for the way we've been living. Even when our current circumstances suggest that we occupy a much smaller place than we desire, the lion or lioness inside of us has to arise and see how great we are. This isn't excessive pride; it's understanding our true identity and purpose and raising our expectations to meet that. Yes, you can learn a lot from a cat—and no, I'm not the crazy cat lady that your crazy neighbor was, so perish the thought!

A popular ancestry.com commercial reveals the importance of how we identify ourselves. A man shares his story, saying, "Growing up, we were German." His family embraced the German culture, danced in a German dance group, and wore lederhosen. When he tested his DNA, he discovered that he was not German at all; most of his ancestry was from Scotland and Ireland. So what did he do then, after the shock wore off? He revealed, "I traded in my lederhosen for a kilt."

It sounds like a cute story promoting ancestry.com. Unwittingly, however, it does more than that. It teaches a lesson. Notice that the man lived according to his presumed identity since his childhood. He was German, or so he thought, so he did things familiar to that culture. When he realized he was something other than he had believed all his life, notice what he did. He changed his garments. He went from the German lederhosen to the Scottish kilt. We can be like that man. If we ever truly grasp our true identity and believe in ourselves, we, too, will cast off the garments we've been wearing—garments of defeat, doubt, and mediocrity. We will take off the old and put on the new—which really isn't new at all. It always was; we just didn't know it, so we lived accordingly.

In this, we see another golden nugget. Some people quote the Bible verse that tells us that the truth makes us free. Amen! But that's just part of it. That verse starts by saying that we "shall know the truth." So we might say that "we shall know the truth, and the truth that we know shall make us free." We need to know it before we can live it, just as we need to know we have money in the bank before we can spend it.

Believe in Your Team

Added to believing in the mission and believing in yourself is believing in your team. When you have a task to tackle, you need to expect that you can complete it successfully. When you are working with others, each person has a role to play, so your level of expectation or confidence is directly proportional to your belief in your teammates. Even if you know that you, individually, are well-equipped, suspecting that others are not will keep you from having high expectations, and that's a problem. "I'm ready! I've got this! I've prepared myself." Well, isn't that special? But look at the people to your left and your right. Are they equally ready? If you are not assured of that, you cannot raise your expectations, which affects your performance.

I used to tell my basketball players that every time they took the court, they had to believe they were the better team and that they were going to win. But there were only two ways for that to occur. One, every player had to know she had done everything she could to prepare to win, and two, every player had to know that everyone else had done everything to prepare to win. If either of those was missing, belief could not be at its maximum; thus, expectation could not, either. As much as some of them played pickup ball in the park or traveled with AAU teams or practiced free throws in their back yards during the off-season, they had to believe their teammates demonstrated the same kind of commitment.

Once again, I have turned to sports to share a lesson, but this also applies to every area that requires collaboration—a school project, a marriage, or a road trip. Yes, a road trip. Most of us won't even close our eyes and rest in a car when we don't trust that the person behind the wheel is a good driver. We may have been driving for eight hours and then switched roles, allowing our friend to take her place as the driver so we can rest for when we have to take over again. But we can't get that rest when we believe the person driving lacks good judgment, cannot see clearly, or is just plain careless. Our expectation of arriving safely is low, if it exists at all. So the formula I have come up with is a simple one to remember: Me + Thee = Expecting Victory. Corny, yes, but nonetheless true.

Speak Life

Speaking life is connected to believing. When we open our mouths, usually what comes out is what's in our hearts. Sure, on occasion, we speak something we don't truly believe, but more often than not, we say it because we believe it. It's one reason public figures are dissuaded from speaking off the cuff; they might actually speak their true feelings, and I guess we wouldn't want that. It's why television personalities get fired and politicians are forced to resign: because they just might have said something that they really believed in an unscripted moment. Scary, I suppose.

Going off teleprompter can lead to going off, period; you just never know what might come out. But ultimately, you cannot man what people speak, even if you monitor what they speak in public. The words we speak to ourselves are just as powerful and have just as much of an effect as the words we speak to others. So the priority is to think and believe right. Then we practice speaking those things because what we say matters. Words are those seeds we discussed earlier. We plant them, we water them, and then we gather their fruit. If they are words of life, that's precisely what we want. However, if they are not, if they are negative, those words are destructive and bring death.

As a teacher, I recognized that the power of my position allowed me to either build up or tear down. I certainly fell short on many occasions, but overall, I was aware that parents had entrusted me with their children; I could use the platform I'd been given to build or to crush. I shared in an earlier chapter that I had a naming ceremony for my students one year, conferring upon them their names and what they mean and charging them to live up to that. I spoke life to them so that they could raise their expectations. It's what Aunt Mary did to me, as you know from the story of how she told my mother to name me Adrienne, following it up with speaking life: her niece would be a teacher.

We have enough wounded people walking around, and, too often, they wound other people. The wise old saying really is accurate: "Hurting people hurt people." We need more whole people, people who have been supported and blessed. We need people who take that positivity and run with it—in the direction of their destinies. If you're a parent, you have the wonderful opportunity to speak life to your child. Educators have that opportunity with their students. Husbands and wives have that opportunity with each other. Neighbors have that with neighbors. There is no shortage of opportunity to speak to others —to speak *into* others—in such a way that their expectations are raised, their hope renewed, and their purpose fulfilled. I mean, we even do it to our pets. How often do we hear, "Good boy"? All the time! So don't tell me you can't encourage and speak life. You do it constantly—often without thinking about it. But we need to think about it, to be purposeful with what we speak to others and what we speak to ourselves. I wonder if we recorded ourselves one day, all day, what we would hear upon playing it back at day's end. Would we find that we are speaking life or death?

As a teacher, I wrote something I entitled the "Declaration of Truth," which, for a time, my students and I recited daily. They loved saying it. Now, some may think that seventh-graders—with all the drama and pressure to be cool that come with those middle school years—were too cool for this. Not so. They asked for it. "We gonna do the 'Declaration of Truth' today, Miss Ross?" I loved it just as much. We all loved it because it made us expectant and hopeful. It spoke to the deep place within us that longs to be inspired. It was lengthy, but it was worth it. All these years later, former students remember it. They don't remember every word of it, but they remember how it made them feel, what it made them believe. Read it and see why:

Declaration of Truth

I am a special individual with a specific purpose for my life. I have been destined for success. I believe that I can fulfill my life's purpose. Failure is not an option. Everything I do prospers. I apply myself, and the result is great accomplishment.

I believe in the success of those around me. I speak good things concerning them, things that lift them up and never tear them down. I am strong in areas where others may be weak. Likewise, my weaknesses are someone else's strengths; therefore, I am not embarrassed or afraid to ask for help. I give help, and I receive help. I understand that whatever I give out will come back to me multiplied.

I do all things with respect. I speak with respect. I listen with respect. I live a life of respect—from the inside out. I honor parents, administrators, teachers, aides, and all those in authority over me.

Tomorrow is not promised. Now is such an important moment in my life. It's the only moment I truly have. I approach it with gratitude, hard work, and faith. No matter what things look like, I refuse to lose, give up, or throw in the towel.

I am unique, wonderfully made, beautiful, and special already—not tomorrow, not when I get straight As, not when I have more friends, or get the things I want. I am already a success. So I will live accordingly—and still, I believe, the best is yet to come.

People have to be spurred on to speak positively. The negative just comes more naturally to us. Perhaps we learn that while growing up listening to our parents or listening to talk radio as adults. The negativity is often so far-fetched we should reject it outright, but because it's popular, I suppose, we gravitate to it. In fact, we often have no tolerance for people who are positive. We distrust them and sometimes even avoid them—finding them irritating. You've heard people say it before: "She's so cheerful, it's annoying!" or "I don't trust him. He's too happy. He must be hiding something." We don't seem to respond the same way to negativity. For example, we don't view with suspicion people who say early in the morning, "He ruined my day." It's 8:00 a.m. How in the world is your day ruined already? Nonetheless, as a teacher, I heard students say that the first thing in the morning. Think about how absurd that is with this scenario: School begins at 8:00 a.m. and ends at 3:00 p.m. Someone or something got under your skin at 8:05 a.m., and you determined then that you're going to have a bad day at school. You have, therefore, made that decision after a mere 1.19 percent of your school day. That's outrageous. To highlight just how outrageous that is, let's apply this same scenario to the years of life. Let's say your life expectancy is 80 years. It would make zero sense if by less than a year, at 11.4 months, you decided your life was no longer worth living because someone had ruined it already.

Those 11-plus months equal 1.19 percent of 80 years. So a student deciding at 8:05 that his seven-hour school day is a wreck and he's just going to be miserable rather than pushing past it is the same as an 11.4-month-old declaring life is a waste and he might as well just die or, at least, remain in the crib. It kind of puts it into perspective, doesn't it?

Adults are no better. Those who are out in the workforce do the same thing when dealing with co-workers as do those who stay at home and deal with their children, spouses, and neighbors. It's unwise and, frankly, unhealthy. Why are we giving that kind of power to people? Disagreements and frustrations occur, but allowing them to dismantle our peace is not what people in control of their destinies do. It's not what people of purpose practice. We take control of our lives and our emotions.

We must live with the expectation of good. Declare the truth. Speak life!

Overcome Obstacles

The final point in raising your expectations is overcoming obstacles. Living an obstacle-free life sounds good, but it's a fantasy. I often tell people if they haven't gone through anything yet, just keep living; it's coming. Everything we have covered so far is good, but stuff happens. And stuff will happen even when you're doing everything possible to soar and when you're dotting and crossing your letters. There's no magic formula to keep us from experiencing life, but using the keys I have shared will help you get through the "stuff" and maybe even minimize it.

I introduced you to my lion-of-a-cat Trooper already. His response to the cracked door teaches us the importance of how we see ourselves. I've learned more from him than that.

I have raised Trooper somewhat like a dog. I treat him like one, and he often acts like one. One thing I do is take him outside every day. Although he would love to be out most of the time roaming, my location is too busy for that—too many cars whizzing by and too many unleashed, unaccompanied animals. But because he loves to be outside and has me wrapped around his paws, I take him out and remain with him. He's never happier than those times, so in all kinds of weather, there I am with Trooper outside. Before we go out, though, I put a harness on him. He doesn't particularly like it, but I do it regularly anyway for an important reason. I first bought the harness, along with a leash, because I was going to teach him how to walk attached to a leash. Let's just say that didn't work out. He may have been raised like a dog, but he knows he's not one, and he was not feeling that leash.

When Trooper is outside without the harness, he's hard to keep up with. He'll take off quickly, try to run freely, and go beyond the boundaries I need him to remain within.

Trooper has adapted somewhat, but initially, when he wore his harness, he became a different creature. He would slink downward and sort of wobble around. He barely wanted to move at all. He would just shrink. It's like life had been completely sucked out of him. His nature was altered for that time. Even now, though he's not quite as bad, he still behaves strangely and inhibited when I put the harness on him, but because he knows he has no choice but to wear it if he wants to go outside, he submits to it. He always resists when he first sees the harness—he does the obligatory walk-away for about three seconds—but he then surrenders so he can get what he wants. When we come back inside, as soon as I remove the harness, he leaps and runs to the room where I keep his food and toys. It's like he's singing, "Free at last! Free at last! Thank God Almighty, I'm free at last!"

As hilarious as his behavior is, it speaks seriously. It shows us what being constricted does. When people ensnare us, put us in their boxes, and control us, it affects our true nature. We were created to be free. That's the longing of every soul. We cannot allow people to make something else out of us, to crush our spirits, to force us in a particular direction for their own purposes rather than supporting our inclination to flourish. Refuse to be harnessed so you can see what you are capable of doing and can have the highest expectations for your life. Cats were not meant to be harnessed. That's why they rebel against it. You were not meant to be harnessed, either. Rebel against it. Trooper does not have a choice. You do.

Make the life-changing decision to raise your expectations right now by acknowledging that you already have accomplishments under your belt and outlining what you feel to pursue next.

Remember, you're still here because you're not done. It's easy to get discouraged or even satisfied. Don't permit the ups or the downs to ensnare you. I use the word "permit" on purpose because entrapment cannot occur without your permission. Give yourself permission to be free to expect more.

Here's the game plan: Believe in the mission, believe in your potential, and believe in your team. Speak life to your vision, your expectation. Refuse to let obstacles deny you. Be active in this pursuit of raised expectations, and you will accomplish greater things than you ever asked or even thought. You'll be able to accomplish what you were meant to accomplish—and not only will you be the better for it, but so will the world to which you have been called.

CHAPTER 9
SHE KILLED HERSELF

If Only I Had Been There

I got the news via a Facebook inbox message. She was dead. That was shocking enough, but the news of how she died followed, and that was earth-shattering. She killed herself—and in the most unimaginable way.

It shook me to my core that a student who sat in my classroom every day found her life so unbearable that she ended it. My heart broke, and I found myself thinking if I had been there, this would not have happened. There is no evidence of that, of course, but I still thought it. By this time, I had moved from New York to Missouri and had transitioned into a new career. I was no longer teaching. I was more than

1,000 miles away and hadn't seen or heard from her since I left the school district. Knowing she had departed from us in this way was too much.

Let me tell you about this student. When I met her, she had what I'd call a "stank" attitude. She turned the eye-roll into an art form. Even when she was silent, the look on her face spoke volumes. It said, "Don't mess with me!" Her silent eye-roll was rivaled only by her loudness in the school hallway when she was with friends.

In spite of her attitude, she and I had a good relationship. She wasn't big on words in class. She was not going to be the first one to raise her hand, and when called upon, she was going to flash a look that said, "Can't you just leave me alone?" But because she liked me and I liked her, she combined that look with a sheepish grin. I could always make her smile in spite of her attitude, which, to be sure, was something to contend with if she didn't like you. Everything she did was in slow motion and methodical, even that smile she flashed at me in class or the hallway. I can still see her in my mind—walking past my room the year after she was in my class, which was her eighth-grade year.

Hearing that she was gone brought all the memories back—her attitude, our relationship, the suppressed smile. But I wasn't there that day to make her smile. She had moved on to the high school, and I hadn't had her as a student since seventh grade, so my contact with her subsequent to that time was minimal. That did not eliminate the thought that I always managed to get her to smile, even hesitantly, and that maybe I could have made a difference.

Her story and stories like it are among the reasons I am passionate about what I do—speaking and writing to inspire. I told an auditorium filled with staff and students in Catskill, New York, that I arrived there with a sense of urgency because, for some of them, the message I was sharing was a life or death one. I said some of them would encounter difficulties in the coming days, and they would have a decision to make. They could throw in the towel, or they could apply the message I was sharing with them—about their true identity and purpose—and persevere. After the presentation, several students approached me to thank me, and some hugged me. This happens often— from students complimenting a speech to expressing gratitude. On two occasions, students confided that a friend in the audience had self-destructive tendencies and needed to hear what I said that day.

It's not just the youth. The adults in the room are among the most moved. There's no age limit for needing inspiration. Just because a speech is geared toward young people doesn't mean adults can't get something out of it. They do. When I speak to adult groups, they grab onto the words, too, and are vocal about what the message meant to them.

We're all different—of different ages, races, proclivities, and experiences—but we each can benefit from a word of truth. I wish I had one more chance to see my former student. I'd do my best to impress upon her how precious she is, how much potential she has, and how far she can go. I'll never have the chance to share that truth, and, apparently, she didn't have it within herself. Oh, how I wish she had known! Heartbreaking.

I recall a time it took forever to get across a bridge I had to travel to get home from work. The cars were piled back for miles, and I didn't know why. This was before everyone carried a cell phone, so there was no one to call to get the lowdown on the holdup. I later learned a man had committed suicide. Eyewitnesses said he was driving across the bridge, stopped his car, got out, walked to the edge, and jumped. No hesitation, no looking back, nothing but stop car, go to edge, jump. Hearing that hit me hard also, and I asked the question I always ask in these situations: could he not find even a sliver of hope? What could be so bad? I say that not to trivialize the real pain people endure, but to ask, "In the midst of it, was there even one thought that tomorrow could be better? Was there one person to take his hand and hold it?" The thought that the answer to those questions was "no" is beyond sad. It ought to make all of us reach out to others and love on them.

Anti-Bullying Bull

"Anti-bullying bull" probably caught your attention, and you're likely to be wondering what it means. I understand. We've gotten so accustomed to the anti-bullying campaigns, literature, and assemblies that we applaud them without consideration that while our motives have merit, our methods are a mess.

I admire the desire to teach young people to respect others and not to mock and demean. I know adults who need to be taught the same thing, by the way. We need to teach children to be kind and not to harass and bully. But even the kindest kid can be cruel at times and, surrounded by his peers, can veer into hurtful behavior. I know parents don't believe that about their kids. Somebody else's kid, yeah, but not theirs. But here's the deal: somebody's kid is bullying somebody else's kid, and when we spot it, we need to deal with it aggressively. It must not be tolerated. Handle it swiftly and sternly. Now that I have made that clear, I will explain why I call the anti-bullying agenda "bull."

You can have all the programs you want, all the laws you want, and all the lectures you want, yet kids will still be kids. A hard fact is that kids often delight in behavior that is typical among their peers, as ugly as it is, and as much as we don't want to admit it. Another fact is that some kids are just flat-out evil. Yes, people can be evil, and children—believe it or not!—are people. You can't legislate enough to keep them from saying things that hurt others. Some just don't care or don't weigh the magnitude of their behavior. The next thing we know, we hear about a child who committed suicide because of the way he was treated or the names she was called. Consequently, we up the anti-bullying programs that didn't work in the first place.

I've said it many times, and I'll say it again: instead of just telling kids not to bully, we need to start telling kids what to do *when* they get bullied because, let's face it—anti-bullying programs and all—kids *will* get bullied. It's not right. It's not fair. But it *is*. Someone somewhere will always bully someone else. So let's take some of those resources spent on the impossible scenario of stopping all people from being jerks and, instead, apply them to the more realistic teaching of how people should handle the jerks they encounter— or, at least, let's balance the message better. Let's help our young people know who they are so they will not fall apart because some classmate said they were not handsome enough or some boy said they were not thin enough. And while we're at it, let's discuss with them how to cope when tough stuff happens anywhere —in the family, in the workforce later, anywhere. They need to know that they can't go around cutting themselves or jumping off bridges or overdosing or anything of the sort when life throws a curveball—a fast curveball. We have to prepare them for those moments, and shame on us if we do not.

So why don't we? In many cases, adults can't deliver the message effectively because too many of us are a mess ourselves. We cannot impart truth and promote healing when we aren't whole ourselves. Oh, we can share information, but information alone won't do it. We don't have to be perfect, because that will never happen, but we need a revelation. We need to have a know-so down inside and a personal conviction that will bring life to others. At every age, at every stage, we need it. This is why an inspirational message meant to uplift youth is the same message that will uplift adults. Many need to hear the same words and are crying out for the same truth. We may have graduated high school already, but we have not yet graduated life, so there are still lessons to receive and apply that will heal fragmented lives in need of repair.

When my former student died, my heart cried out that if I had still been in New York in my old school district, she would not have ended her life. I know that's too much responsibility for one human being to assume. Only God is in all places at all times. He alone is the answer, but we do have opportunities to be His hands and feet and help others. I want to do that. Not that I have arrived and have it all together. That's far from true. Like everyone else who has ever written a book or preached a sermon or volunteered somewhere, we all have our issues, but the Godrevelations of what purpose is, who we really are, and the possibilities before us go a long way to not only make us whole ourselves, but enable us to help others embrace wholeness as well.

Unbandaged but Broken

I made a point of emphasizing that we adults are just as in need of a message of inspiration as youth are. Even with our professions, our families, and our vacations, many of us struggle with identity. Imagine that: Thirty and still trying to find out who we are. Forty and not yet fulfilled. Single and not quite satisfied. Married and "I'm just missing something." Even many who describe themselves as happy lack hope that it can be even better. All the while, we walk around like we have it all together, putting on an act that has become second nature. Some are so good at fronting that they can no longer discern between who they are and the character they have created; it's all intertwined. We have learned to cope, to be successful, and, really, to be all right. I'm not talking about closet pill-poppers or chronically depressed people. I'm talking about most of us. I'm talking about your everyday, average person—the doctor who does your X-rays; the dentist who cleans your teeth; the accountant doing your taxes; and yes, in some cases, the preacher preaching your sermons. No one is above needing a revelation of the potential we have and who we were designed to be, and no one is above being reminded.

No doubt, some who knew my former student from a distance, upon hearing the sad news, thought, "I had no idea." Those who knew the man who jumped off the bridge may have thought the same. We miss so much along the way. We not only miss things in others' lives, but we miss things in our own lives as well.

David Cordeau, who was my pastor several years ago, often shared a fitting illustration. A man broke his arm, went to the doctor, and received a cast. After some time, his doctor removed the cast, and the man went about life as he had always known it. Anyone who saw him noticed the cast was now off and may have even remarked about how good his arm looked. One day, by mistake, someone banged into that arm, and he cried out in pain. Why would contact with the newly unbandaged arm elicit such a response? The answer is obvious: the arm wasn't fully healed. Something, clearly, was not quite right.

That arm looked good as new. It had even returned to its former function of doing what arms do. "Nice arm, nice arm," one might have said. But that arm didn't feel so nice when someone rammed into it.

Our lives are like this. We look like everything is fine. People may comment about how put-together we are. We may even believe it ourselves. Then, bang! Someone gets a little too close to some area of our lives that seemed to be in great shape. She steps hard on our metaphorical toes. She rubs us the wrong way. Maybe she says something in just a certain way. And that's all it takes. It's on! What happened? She awakened the pain in our "arm," and we cried out. What that looks like depends. It could be cursing a person out, flashing a look that could kill, giving the silent treatment, or employing subtle sarcasm. There is always some kind of reaction. Sometimes, the wrong was so slight it should have been ignored. But even if it appears to have warranted a reaction, that reaction reveals that something is going on under the surface. The truth is the situation to which we seem to be reacting is, at times, not the situation to which we actually are reacting. How many people are weighted with something that occurred long before they met us? How many times does someone kindly say, "Good morning!" only to hear, "Really? What's so good about it?" in response? How many men and women pay the price for the infidelity of other men and women? They are distrusted, though they have done nothing wrong.

Yes, we cry out in situations that have nothing to do with those situations at all. We're crying out about another time and place, about things hidden under the surface—some buried deep and some right under the skin. That yelp is what not being whole produces, and it's why we must know that our current and past circumstances do not define who we are and what our futures will be. It's not enough to have a pretty arm. We need a healed arm—one that is not bandaged *and* not broken.

That same pastor used to share another scenario everyone needs to hear. Allow me to share it this way: Busy street. Cries for help. Snarling, vicious dog. Not a peaceful scene. People look up to see a dog ripping a man's leg to pieces, blood dripping to the ground. Some try to distract the dog. Others try to swat him with purses, canes, and burnt pizza crusts they were ingesting while having a walking lunch before the attack caught their attention. Nothing dissuades Fido from devouring the tasty leg, and the man is begging for help, howling in pain, and trying to wrest his body from the hairy, hungry beast.

"We need a bandage!" someone in the crowd yells. "Somebody bring a bandage!" Shortly after, a woman busts through the crowd at full sprint, hoisting a medical kit. "Outta my way!" the brave woman demands, unafraid that Fido will turn on her. She pulls out a bandage, grabs the man's leg, and shares the space with the dog. Holding tightly to the leg the dog has yet to release, the woman begins to wrap the bandage around the bloodiest area while the victim continues to struggle and scream.

Now, how realistic is that? Some of it is, of course. We can imagine a busy street, a hungry dog, and a bloody man. We can imagine the cries for help and the attempts to assist. But that's where it ends. No one would ever do what this woman did. Everyone knows it's insane to bandage the leg until they get the dog off. Get the dog off first. Then tend to the leg.

People spend years bleeding—attacked by insecurities, abuse, rejection, low expectations, pride, anger, you name it. Hounded by what they've decided are failures, they are torn apart and suffer greatly, often in silence. Some of the loudest cries never make a sound. The wound is deep and in need of repair, and they tend to it by masking it, covering it up. Dealing with the symptom of our situation without dealing with the cause is futile. Let's be honest about what's making us cry out and allow the truth to heal us. We are not useless, nor are we hopeless. We are not washed up, nor will we give up. We will not wear garments that tie us to a false identity. No matter how low we've fallen or how high we've climbed, we raise our expectations because we know greater things are ahead. We are still here. We will not be defined by our past; we build on that past as we step into the future.

That is what living life on purpose is all about. In some ways, it just seems like common sense, but in other ways, it just does not come naturally. This dilemma has much to do with habit. We have been trained to think a certain way; therefore, we live a certain way. When that way is a lifelong journey where we embrace hope, purpose, and joy, it's wonderful. However, when it's a journey of despair, doubt, and death, it's tragic.

Thank God, most people do not kill themselves, unlike my former student, whose smile I remember well, who had her whole life ahead of her but did not see its value. Too many of us still are not living, though. We're walking around with pretty arms and bandaged legs—dragging a dog down the street. It's time to reject the familiarity of that, exchange it for true life based on a realization that there's a reason why we're here. There's a reason to get up in the morning and meet the world. There's a reason for persevering through the muck and mire we encounter along the way as we endeavor to fulfill our reason for being. We really do not have time to waste. Young, old, and everyone in between, it's time to live. Not just exist. Live.

CHAPTER 10

FAMILIAR TERRITORY

It seems like a no-brainer that anyone in a bad situation would want out of it, but we know that it doesn't always go down that way. Pain can become as familiar as joy, and people sometimes choose the familiar pain they have over the unfamiliar joy they might find. It's why some people sabotage every good thing that comes their way. Let a woman who is not used to being treated like the queen she is gain the attention of a good-looking, hard-working, supportive man. We think she would say, "It's about time!" and enjoy every moment, but the opposite sometimes occurs instead. She considers him a chump or questions his motives, not having ever encountered the love of a real man who doesn't need to tear her down to build himself up. She expects him to wake up any day and decide that she's not who he thinks she is and then abandon her. Before he gets a chance to drop her, she's determined to destroy the relationship. It seems less painful that way. She would rather go back to the agony of being undervalued because at least then she knows what she's got, and she's accustomed to it. It's familiar in the same way that an old shoe is. It just fits. It's like people say, "Better the devil you know than the devil you don't."

I'm sure you've walked into a college boy's room that smelled like funk or got a whiff of feet that would put corn chips to shame. You can't imagine how the stinky-foot culprit or the funky-room freshman could be oblivious, but he is. Funk that has become familiar ceases to be funk. It's just the norm.

When I go to the salon to get my hair done, I hear a sound over and over again. "Beep! Beep! Beep!" Every few seconds, there it goes. I experienced the same sound at my friend Kia's house. "Beep! Beep! Beep!" I recognized it right away, and it threatened to drive me up the wall. You know what I'm talking about. It's those maddening smoke detectors when the battery begins to bite the dust.

I guess something about me says, "Beep me!" because I also had a neighbor who was never home whose alarm would go off repeatedly. I left a note, knocked on the door, everything. Still "Beep! Beep! Beep!" I finally contacted the landlord because I was going insane and was ready to put my head through the wall. My landlord graciously took care of it for me. The neighbor wasn't home, so we have to excuse him for allowing the beeping to continue—but Kia and my hairstylist? When I asked them about it, wondering how in the world they could ignore the sound, the answer was, "What sound?" They had become so familiar with the noise the detector made, they no longer heard it.

The salon was the worst because it had two detectors that, over time, were in competition with one another. One had already been beeping in the back, where my stylist did my hair, but now, another was beeping in the front, where she ran a beauty supply store, and they took turns tormenting me. We laughed about it for months because every time I returned to get my hair done, there was the beeping, only now, instead of "Beep! Beep! Beep!" it was "Beep-Beep! Beep-Beep! Beep-Beep." And I was going, "Just kill me! Just kill me! Just kill me! If you like me at all, please put me out of my misery, and just kill me!"

People became deaf to the sound because the sound had become a permanent part of their surroundings. It was one with them.

Being around a stench means we're dragging it with us wherever we go. Who hasn't experienced cooking fish or fried chicken, eating it, then realizing in an embarrassing moment that though you have left the house, the smell that was in the house hasn't left you? That can be a problem. We may love to eat that food, and it sure does taste good, but do we really want to show up somewhere smelling like fish? It doesn't take long for the smell to cling to you, and it may take someone telling you that you smell like fish before you even realize it.

Sometimes, a good smell lingers on us. When we've been in the presence of someone wearing an appealing perfume, it gets on us. We may not realize it at first. Someone may say, "Hey, you smell like Liz" or "You smell like Donny." Liz and Donny are identified by a scent because people have gotten used to the fragrance they often wear. Their scent becomes our scent, but that, too, can become a problem.

We understand why we want to avoid stinky smells that cling to us, but we may struggle a bit trying to understand what's bad about a good smell. It's bad when someone else's scent competes with our scent. Our lives exude their own fragrance. It helps set us apart. We need to allow that unique part of who we are to shine and not be overridden by someone else. We should all have role models, but let's be careful not to lose ourselves. Have you ever seen people who have studied someone so much that they gesture like them, talk like them, and even walk like them? They lose themselves in someone else, and it all gets blurred. The other person becomes so familiar that the person we are is lost. This is unhealthy.

The danger of becoming attached to people who aren't good for us is that after a while, we feel at home and cease to recognize the good from the bad or, more tricky, the good from the best.

Then we have the situation of marriage, where two people are supposed to be familiar with one another. A husband and wife should know each other better and more intimately than anyone else. That's what marriage is about—two lives becoming one. The prospect of that sparks an excitement in people from their childhood. Girls, especially, are known for dreaming about the Big Day—the wedding day. I've known people who had their dresses mentally designed when they were barely teenagers. They knew who their bridesmaids would be, what kind of cake they would have, the songs they wanted sung. They knew it all—except who the groom was. I guess in the big scheme of things, that's minor. Okay, probably not. The point is they had their weddings planned.

Stereotypically, men don't quite approach marriage the same way. They don't spend years jotting down notes for their wedding day; instead, they tend to make jokes about the old ball and chain. One thing we hear, though, is that when a guy finds Ms. Right, it's a wrap. He's hooked. It may take a while to get him to that point, but when he gets there, stick a fork in him; he's done.

During the courting period, the two lovebirds cannot get enough of gazing into each other's eyes. She will do anything for him, and he will do anything for her. Nothing is an inconvenience. He surprises her with flowers. She cooks his favorite meals. Her best friends are upset with her because she no longer has time for movie night, and his brothers are ticked that he blows off pickup basketball—or vice versa. They love learning about each other, sitting quietly, talking.

Let her feet hurt, and he'll rub them. Let his scalp itch, and she'll scratch it. Anything!

And then they get married.

After the "I do," honeymoon, and a little time together, things begin to change. What was once a pleasure becomes a pain. The smile that was like sunshine doesn't manifest as often. The food that evoked, "Thank you for making this for me, baby" barely gets an acknowledgment. The figure once admired goes unnoticed. They argue—or at least disagree—over the smallest things. They have lost that first love. How? They grew familiar with each other. They began to live out the adage: "Familiarity breeds contempt."

Of course, this does not happen with everyone. I've seen couples married for 40 years who not only love each other still, but they even like each other. They serve each other. They sacrifice for each other. He treats her like his princess, and she honors him like her prince. It's a sight to behold. But too often, this is not the case. Too often, the excitement dies where the pursuit is buried. She had wanted him, and he had wanted her. Once she had him and he had her, they took each other for granted. They became familiar, comfortable, and they no longer appreciated or even noticed the things that once made their hearts skip a beat. Divorce court is filled with stories like this.

Various scenarios arise that reveal the effect the familiar has on us. Let's endeavor to be familiar with who we are, our best selves. Let's not get lost because our senses have grown stale. Let's stay awake and alive to what is before us, cherishing each person and each moment without losing ourselves and our purpose in the process.

Did you notice my word choice? I chose words and phrases that conjure up images of action. Go back and look at them: "endeavor," "not get lost," and "stay awake." These words highlight the responsibility that we have. We have choices to make. If we are not intentional with our own lives, we will find ourselves in the same place year after year. A huge part of the battle is understanding that things don't just flow or roll on their own most of the time. *We* put the ball in motion. Even the things we call God-things are often the culmination of the steps of faith we have taken along the way. We must choose not to get stuck in that snug, comfy place just because we know it so well.

It boils down to this for me: I don't want to walk around oblivious to sounds to which I've grown accustomed. I don't want to stink because a stench became a part of me. I don't even want to emit someone's pleasant fragrance to the point that when people see me, they think of that other person. No, I want to find out who I am, what I'm supposed to do, and live it. I want to be so familiar with my purpose that while I learn from other people—and I must—I apply valuable lessons to my own life that help me blossom into a first-class me, not a second-hand someone else.

CHAPTER 11

BE OPEN

Earlier, I discussed keys to determining your purpose. One key is your passion. In this chapter, I want to emphasize that there are times when we shy away from all things that are uncomfortable, things that we are not passionate about and cannot imagine ourselves involved in. Though we must consider our passions when considering our purpose, know that a lack of desire or passion today does not mean that the desire won't come at some point.

For the longest time, I could never have imagined myself in the mountains of Guatemala. Not me! My church was a missions-minded church, so much so that my pastor, Pastor Jaron Halsted, used to say—only half-jokingly—that anyone who wanted to be a part of our congregation would be required to get a passport because we were not going to sit around and just be good Americans. No, we were going to go on the mission field, see what it was like to spend time in another culture, and help others who could never repay us. Our church was connected to several ministries and went annually to Guatemala and Zambia. Mission teams also went to Mississippi to help after Hurricane Katrina. But foreign missions was a regular. Teams of all ages would set out to build, minister, and love on people—and I had zero interest in going overseas.

Guatemala was always a difficult trip, judging from the stories. Those who went came back changed and loved the experience, but it was no cake-walk. I remember my pastor encouraging me to go on a mission trip, and I remember thinking, "Yeah, right!" As far as I was concerned, I didn't mind helping in the United States, but I was not planning on going out of the country for a mission trip. Pastor Jaron even suggested that I start my mission experience with Africa, as it was a less demanding experience than Guatemala. I had for some time thought of visiting Africa, but going on a mission trip there was not in my plans, and I was not really open to the idea.

My not being open to going was not the end of the story, however. Out of the blue, it seemed, my heart began to change. I remember all of a sudden having a stirring to go across the world and serve. That was weird. The desire was so intense that the year before I went, as the group that was about to head out to Guatemala lined up in front of the church so we could pray for them and send them out, I was almost jealous that I wasn't going with them. Who would've thought? I certainly had never experienced that. I remember consoling myself: "Next year, Adrienne."

If I based whether I was meant to go into the mission field on how I originally felt about it, I would never have gone. When the desire began to rise within me, I would have dismissed it as just me. I would have suppressed it. I had to be open, however, to the idea that something was transpiring within me that was larger than I.

I later learned that Pastor Jaron had been praying for me about missions. He told me, "You said you were not going, and telling you that you needed to go wasn't doing any good. Sometimes, you have to be quiet and just pray, so I prayed." So much wisdom is in those words. We often try to manipulate people into doing what we want them to do. Maybe it's something we know they need to do. But poking and prodding do not change people's hearts or drive them to their purpose. In fact, it sometimes does the opposite; it causes them to resist and retreat. Instead of trying to force people, taking your hands off the situation can yield amazing results. My pastor decided he was going to let God do it. He somehow knew that the plan for my life called for the mission field, so what did he do? He backed off and just prayed. God changed my heart along the way. I became open to the idea, though the details didn't sound pleasant. Then, I went. Not only did I go to Guatemala, but no sooner had I returned than I started preparing for my next mission trip—this time to Africa—and seven months later, I was there.

Africa was another amazing experience. The people are the most beautiful—both outwardly and inwardly. Like Guatemala, it took me out of my comfort zone, stretched me, and changed my view of the world. I realized how blessed I was, but I also realized how blessed the people of Africa were. They didn't have the material things we had, but they had joy anyway. They were generous people. Americans are charitable also, but sometimes, we hold back because we feel we don't have enough. These people wanted to give. It was their way of expressing how much they appreciated that we came there to help them. My heart was torn because they wanted to give away jewelry, clothing, anything that they valued, as tokens of their gratitude. I couldn't wrap my brain around accepting from them. I asked Pastor Jaron what I should do. "Pastor, they're trying to give me their things. What do I do?" His response: "Receive it." I had to learn to receive from them because they wanted to give. It meant so much to them to give whatever they could. While there, we helped build a church, ministered on the streets and at church, entertained children at an orphanage, held an assembly at a school, and visited hospitals, praying for people who had malaria, AIDS, and other illnesses. Yet the people we went to serve gave us much more than we gave them. We learned more from them than we taught them. Had I not been open to going, I wouldn't have had the opportunity to grow the way I did.

I came back to my job at the school and organized assemblies replete with pictures, videos, and stories, sharing the experience with my students and community so they, too, would be inspired—and they were.

I hear people say they will never go on a mission trip, and I'm reminded that I used to say the same. I long for them to be open to breaking out of that familiar place and allowing themselves to expand rather than choosing to remain in safe waters at the shore.

Consider slavery. We would have never heard of Harriet Tubman, conductor of the Underground Railroad, had she remained where it was safe. You assert the slave plantation was not safe at all, and I can appreciate that point. It was hard work, long hours, and ungodly slave masters. It was the whip, the scorching sun, and horrid conditions. After all, it was slavery, not something we associate with safety. But it *was* safe—in the sense that it provided a place with which to identify; food to eat, though hardly enough; and a routine, as ghastly as it was. Beyond the plantation were more questions than there were answers and certainly no guarantees. So for Tubman to choose to leave the only life she had known on a quest for the vague notion of freedom almost defied all reason. However, for her, managing to envision life apart from slavery and recognizing that "slave" was not her true identity were nothing if not reasonable. Tubman not only made her way North, but reportedly, in a ten-year period, she made 19 trips back to the South and guided more than 300 slaves to freedom, including her sister, her two nieces, and her parents.

History tells us that Tubman "never lost a single passenger." That does not mean that no one was tempted to give up—to lie down and die or to go back to the familiar; escape had to be the hardest thing they ever attempted. Persisting on the uncertain, dangerous road to freedom was harder than the hell of slavery. Some grew weary along the way and were ready to turn back. History also tells us that Tubman would not allow them to retreat. She got her stellar record of never losing a passenger because she forced them to persevere by threatening them with a firearm. You read that right. She is quoted as saying, "You'll be free or die." Talk about pressure.

One might say, "Hey, if they wanted to go back, she should have let them go back. That's their bad fortune. We're out!" But there was more to it than that.

First, if they turned back, they would probably be forced to spill the beans and reveal the path the others had taken. That would have been an end to the Underground Railroad and put the lives of those who helped in jeopardy. They could not risk that.

The next, probably more important, point was that she knew that their getting to the promised land would take someone stronger than themselves. It would take someone pushing them past the breaking point, someone who said, "I want this for you more than you want this for yourself, and I'm not going to let you quit." Her actions said, "I'll threaten to kill you before I'll let you kill your dream, your birthright, your identity, and your purpose." The slaves, perhaps, would hate her at that moment, but the moment they crossed into freedom, they would thank her. She knew this to be true, and in her own way, she tweaked Patrick Henry's "Give me liberty or give me death!" to "I'll give you liberty or I'll give you death!" Everyone on the journey received liberty. They took a chance. They may have taken one long look back, but they bid farewell to the familiar, opening up to the possibilities of something they had not been able to conceive because they had no frame of reference. Something within said they were born for this, and they went after it on the Underground Railroad with Tubman. Every one of them reached it, thanks to their conductor.

"When I found I had crossed that line, I looked at my hands to see if I was the same person. There was such a glory over everything; the sun came like gold through the trees, and over the fields, and I felt like I was in Heaven." Tubman reportedly said this about her successful journey to freedom. I find it most interesting that coming into her true identity affected her so profoundly that she had to look at herself to see if she was the same person because even her skin seemed to have changed. Her view of the world changed. Everything was brighter. This was the closest thing to Heaven she had ever experienced, both externally and internally. She became, in that moment, what she was always meant to be: free. I know it's true because had she not believed there was more for her than the slave plantation, she would never have left it.

I greatly admire Tubman's selfless commitment to dangerously return so others could taste the freedom she could have safely settled into herself. We do that a lot: "I got mine. See if you can get yours. You're on your own." Instead, Tubman was open to risk so others could have reward. The beauty of this message of identity and purpose is that finding yours makes you want others to find theirs. You want to help. That's why I share my story and speak to youth and encourage adults. This is too good to keep to myself. I don't have it all together. Not even close. I'm open to more, and I'm excited knowing more is coming because this is a journey, not a destination. I don't have every piece to this puzzle of life. But I have *something* to share. I have revelation that will help someone else. And as long as God allows, I will reach out to others, and I will delight in seeing them embrace what He has for them.

Oh, and by the way, the woman we know as Harriet Tubman was born with a different last name: Ross. I learned many years ago that my family bloodline includes the family of Harriet Ross Tubman. This family history nugget both humbles me and makes me proud. It is an honor to read her story and to realize that what she did so dramatically in leading people to freedom from slavery is what I am doing on a smaller, no less significant, scale: leading people to personal freedom.

FINAL THOUGHTS

We get one shot at life on earth. Just one. That's a tough pill to swallow because for as long as we can remember, people have preached to us about "second chances" and "try, try again." While life is made up of parts we perfect, lessons we learn, and wrongs we right, life itself is a one-fer, a fast one at that. It goes quickly. The sooner we learn to embrace its purpose, the more time we have to live that purpose, and the more fulfilled we are.

If you're reading this page, it's because you found the message in this book worth your time and attention. I believe you found inspiration on every page, some keys to help you move into your purpose, and a vision of what that looks like. It's time to do something about it. Don't let pain stop you, low expectations derail you, or the opinions of others harness you. Even if you're not sure what your purpose is, you know you have one. You know there's something more. That's why you picked up this book. That's why you're reading it. That's why even when you are confused or weary or just want a little something-something more, you don't give up.

I have shared no sob story. This message of purpose is just as vital to those who are on top of the world as it is to those who feel the world is on top of them. No matter where you stand, there's a higher place to go, and there are ways to get there. Allow the truth to spur you. Let your faith elevate you. And permit your purpose to propel you. There's so much more. Obstacles will emerge, but failure is not an option, and suicide is not a solution. The challenges are just part of your journey and part of your story. It's difficult to receive inspiration from someone who has never had to endure anything. We love overcoming the odds movies. We love rags to riches stories. We even love riches to more riches stories if they have a human frailty element.

Don't judge whether you're on the right road by the road itself. Different roads have different terrain at different locations. Keep your eyes on your road, your purpose. Determine now that when the ground gets bumpy, you'll carry on. There's freedom to be gained.

And if you're already there, if you're soaring like an eagle, raise your expectations. You still have breath, which means there's more for you—if not to receive, then to give. Someone needs you to be a Harriet Tubman in his life. Someone needs you to refuse to let her turn back.

When I was almost done writing this book, I needed to get away to put a dent in it. I planned for weeks to drop Trooper off at a friend's house. He loves Aunt Kristi and goes on play dates at her house so he can torment—I mean play with!—her cat, Rootie. He was going to spend the weekend there, and I was going to be in a hotel room wrapping up this book. It didn't work out as planned.

At the last minute, the temperature dropped drastically, which meant that Jersey, Kristi's dog, would have to be inside the house. Rootie and Jersey were used to the routine and had learned how to carefully, if begrudgingly, co-exist. Trooper had never been in that situation. This could be a bad scene. I was crushed because I wanted to finish the book and get it into your hands. I knew it would bless you, and I was up against a deadline. I refused to cancel my plans. I was fixed on finishing what I started, and I was fixed on getting as close as possible to doing so that weekend.

I called the hotel and learned that they allowed pets, so rather than scrapping my idea, I put the infamous harness on my cat, secured his cat seatbelt that attaches to his harness, and hit the road with Trooper. I refused to be denied. Trooper travels well in a car, but to go to the front desk, hotel rules dictated that he be confined in a carrier. That was a trip! Trooper hates that thing, and it was a nightmare getting him in there. He howled and whined, and the hotel lobby noise frightened him. Once in the hotel room, he was still beside himself. He found a safe space and would not come out. It broke my heart, but in time, he ventured out and became comfortable. He noticed the large window, and by jumping on the heater, he could look outside at all the comings and goings.

Those I shared the story with afterwards looked at me as if to say, "You took your cat?!" I sure did!

Why am I sharing this? Because isn't this just like life? You plan everything meticulously, but it often doesn't turn out the way you planned. We can then throw in the towel and say, "Oh, well. I guess it wasn't meant to be" or "I give up." Those are options. But there's another one: to plod ahead—to see the bump in the road and reroute. I've often heard people say that with God, life is like a GPS. It's impossible to get lost with that gadget. Try to get lost by taking a different route than it gives you. Instead of saying, "Go back home. This ain't working," that GPS will say, "Proceed to the route." When you continue to go a different way—maybe because that route is closed, you're confused, or an obstacle exists—it will say, "Rerouting." Be willing to reroute. You'll get there.

It was stressful adding Trooper to the plan. In fact, one reason I planned to get away was to get away from Trooper so I would be unhindered. But life doesn't work out that way sometimes. I did reroute, but I did not give up, and I accomplished more that weekend than I had accomplished in months.

The weather was the monkey wrench in my plan. I don't know what your monkey wrench is that tries to deter you from what you want to accomplish—what you were created to accomplish—but whatever it is, don't let it win. I don't know what your Trooper is— the thing you didn't expect to have to contend with on your journey—but deal with it. When you feel like screaming, "I can't want to!" do it anyway.

I have prayed for every person who will read this book, and I believe your destiny is success. You will fulfill your purpose in all of its uniqueness. It won't look like anyone else's, so get that out of your head. Do *you*! Do what *you* were created to do. Be who *you* were meant to be. You're worth the effort. So push your way to purpose.

MEET THE AUTHOR

ADRIENNE ROSS is an author, editor, columnist, speaker, and former teacher and coach. She taught English in the Hudson City School District in Hudson, New York, for 17 years and now owns Adrienne Ross Communications.

Adrienne is a dynamic speaker and uses this gift in presentations to schools, churches, political groups, national and international service organizations, and businesses.

Adrienne is the author of *#AuntAlma: Raisin' a Little ~~Hell~~ Heaven on Earth* and *#AuntAlma Unleashed: Old, Bold, and Out of Control*. Both are illustrated, humorous books filled with the unique wisdom of her aunt, Alma Ross.

Adrienne is passionate about pursuing her purpose and encourages others to pursue theirs as well.

Contact Adrienne Ross by visiting her websites: adriennerosscom.com and auntalma.com.

CONTACT THE AUTHOR

Schedule Adrienne Ross to speak
at your event or purchase her books in bulk:

adriennerosscom.com

auntalma.com

adriennerosscom@gmail.com

Made in the USA
Middletown, DE
21 July 2017